NAMES FOR LIGHT

Also by Thirii Myo Kyaw Myint

The End of Peril, the End of Enmity, the End of Strife, a Haven

NAMES FOR LIGHT

A Family History

THIRII MYO KYAW MYINT

Graywolf Press

Early versions of portions of the Sittwe section and portions of the second _____ section appeared in *Territory*.

This publication is made possible, in part, by the voters of Minnesota through a Minnesota State Arts Board Operating Support grant, thanks to a legislative appropriation from the arts and cultural heritage fund. Significant support has also been provided by the National Endowment for the Arts, Target Foundation, the McKnight Foundation, the Lannan Foundation, the Amazon Literary Partnership, and other generous contributions from foundations, corporations, and individuals. To these organizations and individuals we offer our heartfelt thanks.

This is a work of creative nonfiction. The events, places, people, and conversations depicted here have been recreated from memory and some have been compressed, summarized, or otherwise altered.

Published by Graywolf Press
250 Third Avenue North, Suite 600
Minneapolis, Minnesota 55401

www.graywolfpress.org

Published in the United States of America

ISBN 978-1-64445-061-1

2 4 6 8 9 7 5 3 1
First Graywolf Printing, 2021

Library of Congress Control Number: 2020944217

Cover design: Kyle G. Hunter

For my family

Contents

I

Leymyethna   5

———————— 15

Gayan   25

Denver   35

Sittwe   45

II

Leymyethna   57

Yangon   67

Minbu   77

South Bend   87

Sittwe   103

III

Hinthada   115

———————— 127

Gayan   139

Madrid   151

Sittwe   165

IV

Hinthada   177

Yangon   189

Minbu   199

Providence   209

Sittwe   221

V

NAMES FOR LIGHT

I

Leymyethna

My great-grandfather died a man but was reborn as me. He died in a small village in the jungle, the son of a princess hiding from war. The village where they hid was called Leymyethna, four faces, a village built around a pagoda of the same name, bearing a four-faced Buddha. It was my great-grandmother's village, the place where she was born.

The city where I was born was also once a place to hide. Yangon, the end of yan, of peril, enmity, strife. It was a place where there were no enemies, where enemies could not follow. Except enemies did follow, so that by the time I was born, the city had been conquered thrice, by the British, the Japanese, and the military junta. Three enemies to symbolize the three torments of the mind: greed, aversion, delusion.

My great-grandfather's death was foretold by a trunk that slipped off a bridge and fell into the river upon the family's arrival in the village. My great-grandfather's trunk, full of his precious things. The son of a princess, my great-grandfather had inherited diamonds and rubies, sapphires and pearls, jewels my mother had never seen but had heard her mother talk about with remorse, for all the jewels were eventually sold, one by one, to educate my great-grandfather's sons.

No jewels were sold to educate my grandmother. She was one of seven children, the eldest daughter, my great-grandfather's favorite child. Her brother, the eldest son, did not call the doctor when my great-grandfather was dying because, my mother said, he resented the love his father had shown only to my grandmother. My grandmother who was born a girl and born second. She was fourteen when her father died, when the cities were bombed, the schools shut down.

Many years after my great-grandfather's trunk fell in the river, my mother dreamed two trunks were thrown into the artificial lake in the center of the city where she had married my father on a floating, mythical bird. My mother was inside of one trunk, my brother in the other, and both trunks were coffins, sinking into the lake, filling up with cold water, and in the dream my mother tried to scream, to break out, she threw her body against the lid of the trunk, kicked and clawed, but it would not open, she could not breathe, until finally, she ceased to struggle, she accepted death, and as she closed her eyes, the trunk opened and her body floated to the surface. Alone in that cold water. When my mother awoke from the dream, she knew that my brother would not live.

Except my brother did live, since he returned as my eldest sister, who was born with a birthmark on her foot in the same spot where my grandfather had placed a thumbprint of ash on my brother's foot before he was cremated.

There are no marks on my body from a previous life. Unlike my eldest sister, I was born perfectly blank, perfectly bare. For years, I waited for a mark to appear, a sign of who I was or had been or would become. I searched my body, read and reread it carefully. The sharp point of a tooth, the shape of my hands, the places where I could not bear to be touched: my back, my pelvis, under my chin. I was afraid to change my body in any way, to leave my own mark upon it. I got no tattoos, no piercings. I never dyed my hair, and the one time I had it chemically straightened, I shaved it off afterward. I believed I had to keep my body plain and pristine if I was to receive a sign.

More than once, I believed I had immaculately conceived a child. It is possible for a body to mimic the conditions of pregnancy if the mind believes, possible for the uterus to expand, for the cervix to soften, for the belly to swell. My belly did not swell, but for several months, I felt nauseated and tender, and did not bleed. Every time I found the blood, on the sheets or on my underwear, it was both a relief and a loss.

And my great-grandfather's trunk was recovered. The trunk that slipped off the bridge and fell into the river. The river was not very wide or very deep, and men from the village dove into the water to retrieve it. The family jewels were saved, to be locked in an attic and eventually sold.

Only my great-grandfather had seen his trunk fall into the water. He had seen it sink beneath the surface, carried away by the current. He could not unsee what he had seen. He knew it was an omen of death.

As a child, I conflated my great-grandfather's body and his trunk of possessions and imagined it was he who slipped off the bridge and fell into the river. I imagined the water turning pink where he hit his head on a rock, the water carrying him away, downstream, then around a bend, so my great-grandmother and grandmother could no longer see him. All rivers lead to waterfalls or to the ocean, so I imagined my great-grandfather was transported somewhere no one could follow him, although my grandmother did try, since she moved south to Yangon, then called Rangoon, a city by the ocean, and my parents and I tried to follow him even farther since we moved across the Pacific. As a child, I imagined that one day my great-grandfather's body would wash up on a beach in Half Moon Bay the way dead whales, jellyfish, and cows sometimes did.

Even when I learned that my great-grandfather had died of a hemorrhagic stroke, a blood vessel that ruptured in his brain, even when I learned that he had died sitting in a chair, not drowning in a river, and that, for my great-grandfather, dying in the jungle, dying in wartime meant dying in the comfortable ancestral home of his wife, the daughter of a village elder, I could not erase the path that the river had carved in my mind. From under the bridge in Leymyethna, south to join the Pathein River, then through the delta into the Pacific Ocean and across it to the shores of Northern California. A path created by my great-grandfather's body, or rather the absence of his body, an absence that I had to fill with my body since I was reborn from him.

I do not know if there really is a four-faced Buddha in the pagoda at Leymyethna. The name alone made me imagine it. Myethna means face or surface, but it could also mean cardinal direction. Maybe there are four Buddhas inside the pagoda, seated back-to-back, facing the four directions, or four Buddhas in each corner of the temple, or four windows to let in varying amounts of light, from the east, west, south, and north.

When I learned the cardinal directions in two languages as a child, I thought the English version made more sense: north, east, south, west. It was satisfying to begin at the top and make my way clockwise, in a circle, as if place and time worked in the same way. In Bamar, I had to make a cross, east to west, and south to north. I understood that the sun rose in the east and set in the west, and that was a day, a measure of time, but I did not understand what the south-to-north axis measured. In my textbook, there was a picture of a little girl with her arms held out to her sides facing the sunrise. The girl seemed to suggest that east to west and south to north intersected only at the origin point of a body. South was inscribed on her right arm, north on her left, and west was on her back, which was to me, the reader. Only east floated on the horizon before her, drawing her gaze and mine.

In a story about the before-and-after life the awakened one asks a girl four questions.

Where do you come from?
Where are you going?
Do you not know?
Do you know?

She answers *I do not know* to all the questions except the third. *Do you not know?* he asks. *I do know*, she says. What she means is, she knows she is going to die.

I know some things as well.

I know, for example, where I was born. I know where I lived from the age of one until the age of seven. I know where I lived from the age of eight until the age of eighteen. I know no one wants to know about the places where I lived after the age of eighteen. No one wants to know about the choices I made. I know that few who ask that question, the first question the awakened one asked the girl, want to hear me speak at all. Most want me only to listen. They want to tell me where I come from. No, not California, but where I really come from, before and before, back and back, to the time when I was still there, and they were already here. I know that is where they think I am from, where they think I still belong—there. Over there. Elsewhere. Far, far away. The place they have never heard of, or they read about once in the news, or their friend visited, or they visited, too, or it was a neighboring country but close enough, they travel a lot, they have seen a lot, they have seen people who look like me.

Sometimes I forget what I look like because I see myself every day. I look in the mirror and I see skin the color of skin, hair the color of hair, eyes the color of eyes. I forget to see what they see: difference, otherness. But I do not forget for long because soon I am told how I look. Soon—at the supermarket, the park, a bar, a clinic, in the back seat of a car—I am looked at, stared at, and commented upon.

The color of your skin and your hair.
You look like you could be.
You look like you aren't.

Then the questions, the same ones every time. Just curious, just out of curiosity. And I am here to satisfy. I am here, in this country, so it is the least I can do. Nod and smile and keep my mouth shut. I want to shut my eyes too because there is nothing to see. Because the ones staring at me are blank, empty, and invisible. The many different colors of their skin become one color that I am not supposed to see, that no one is supposed to see, a color that absorbs no visible light, reflects them all back.

Where do you come from? he asks the girl. *I do not know*, she says, and he knows exactly what she means. She does not have to explain. The awakened one cannot read minds, but he does have perfect wisdom.

I was born in Yangon, the capital. From the age of one until the age of seven I lived in Bangkok, a different capital of a different nation. In the old days, the two nations were always at war and the boundary between them was always moving, shifting east or west as kingdoms rose and fell. In the old days, a new capital was founded each time a new king came into power. Palaces were destroyed by armies, earthquakes, left to crumble, or dismantled, moved, and rebuilt. *In the old days*, I say, though I know days do not age, but simply begin and end. *The young days*, I should say, the days that passed quickly, the days that passed away, that died young. The dead days. And it is true those days are dead: the kings whose beautiful names I learned are dead, the queens whose names I did not learn are dead, the laborers who built their palaces are dead. Before I turned eight, my family moved away from capital cities forever to a place with strip malls, ranch-style houses, and foothills in every direction.

It was a place I had no name for, still have no name for. San Jose, Cupertino, Saratoga, Silicon Valley, South Bay, Bay Area. None of these names could hold the place together for me. It was a place without a center, a city that did not surround. As one drives through, the streets change their names and change them again, but remain the same. I never dream of this place. This place where I lived from the age of eight until the age of eighteen, this place where my parents still live, this place I return to twice a year, this place I say I come from.

This place repeated enough times begins to sound like *displaced*.

Displaced is where we moved to, displaced is where I grew up, displaced is where I am from.

There is a city I have dreamed of for as long as I can remember. It is not Bangkok or San Jose or Providence or Madrid or South Bend or Denver. It is not any other city I have passed through or visited. The dreams always begin with my body moving through space, walking or running across a wide street, the roof of a building. It is gray in the city, always dim, neither night nor day. The light is artificial, fluorescent; I do not know where it comes from because I never look up. In my dreams, I take the city for granted. It is the place where I am and have always been, too familiar to be looked at. The other people in the city form a collective body and move together as one mass. I do not look at them either. I do not know if they look like me, or if I look like them. In my dreams that does not matter. What matters is that I do what I have to do.

My goals are so simple I can never remember them when I wake up. A question to answer, something to find, a person to meet. When the dreams begin, I am confident I will accomplish these tasks quickly and easily. I am so confident I allow myself to be distracted, to delay and explore a bit. That is when the dreams change, when the city becomes a maze. Familiar streets do not lead where they should, landmarks disappear. I take a wrong turn and then I take another one. Sooner or later, I am lost. Night falls and the crowds thin. I do not know where I am, but know I am far from where I'm meant to be. I know I am moving farther away still.

In these dreams, I never think, *I want to go home. I want to give up this task and go home.*

I have no home in the dream city. I never dream of a place to re-turn to. The city itself is where I live, the streets, the alleyways, the secret stairs and passages that only I can find. At the end of the dreams, when I am frustrated, when I am scared and beginning to panic, it never occurs to me to find shelter, to rest. I only think, *I want to be there already.* The place where I am meant to be, the place I have not reached yet, the unknown. That is the place I yearn for.

In the story about the before-and-after life, the girl has no name. She is called only the girl, the maiden, or the weaver's daughter. The girl has no mother either, only a father, the weaver. The girl works in the weaver's shop. That is why she was late to the awakened one's talk.

The girl's mother died when the girl was young, and her mother's death was the girl's first memory. Or the girl's mother died giving birth to the girl, so the girl grew up knowing she was born from death. Or the girl's mother died not long before the awakened one came to their town, so the girl had lately been thinking of death. *Life is uncertain, death is certain, life ends in death.* When the awakened one asks the girl the four questions, she knows what she does and does not know. She does not know what came before birth, or what comes after death. She knows she will die. She does not know when or how or where. The point of the story is that no one knows. We are all just making it up. Beginning and ending and beginning again.

After her encounter with the awakened one, the girl returns to the weaver's shop. Struck on the breast by her father's loom, she falls down dead. Her father and the townspeople are chastened.

Gayan

In another small village surrounded by another jungle, another great-grandfather dies an early death. I do not know as whom or what, or where he is reborn. My father does not claim to know either. There are thirty-one planes of existence and humans dwell in only one.

The village where my great-grandfather died is called Gayan, a very small village by the Irrawaddy River, just before it reaches the sea. It is the same village where my great-grandfather was born. His family had been the most prosperous one in the village, the largest landowners. My great-grandfather died because his family lost their land, because he had to sell their land to keep his sister's husband out of jail. In those days, my father said, a man could be thrown in jail for not paying his debts. My great-grandfather's sister did not want her husband thrown in jail, her husband who bought rice when the price was low and sold it when it was high. He was a gambler, my father said, which was not an honest way to earn a living.

My great-grandfather earned his living through the land he owned, land that was farmed by men, women, and children who did not own it, who would never come to own it, no matter how hard they worked. They rented the land from my great-grandfather and paid him in crops and money made from the sale of the crops. I do not think it was not an honest way to earn a living either.

When my great-grandfather sold the land, not to these families who had been farming it for years, but to the debt collectors, he was left with only a plot of land for himself. A family farm, which he would have to work with his own hands. My great-grandfather could not do it. He did not know how to earn a living with his hands, with his body, how to make a life.

So, he died, my great-grandfather, the father of my father's father. And I am sorry I have broken this chain of fathers and sons by being born a daughter. I am sorry that my brother died. My brother and my great-grandfather are both remembered only for their deaths. My brother died in infancy, at the beginning of his life. My great-grandfather, at least, had a chance to live, to become a man and a father, to raise five sons.

Of the five, my father says, apart from my grandfather, their lives did not go so well.

The eldest died from injuries sustained in a street fight, soon after their father's death.

The second eldest became a gangster.

The fourth went AWOL, was caught, and imprisoned.

The youngest died young of illness.

As the third son, the one in the middle, my grandfather held his brothers' diverging lives together. He was the one recurring character in all the stories that my father told us, my sisters and me, of our great-uncles and their misadventures. The story about the sampan that was hijacked by guerillas and later sunk in the ocean. The story about the horse-cart business and the drunk Japanese soldiers who put an end to it. The story about the cousin who got pregnant out of wedlock and the family feud that started on her behalf. My grandfather always played a minor role in these stories; he was always the observer, the outsider looking in. As a child, I was not interested in him. It was my great-uncles whom I loved to hear about. The second uncle, whose name meant ten thousand, and the fourth, whose name meant one hundred thousand. They were both tricksters, foolish as often as they were cunning, unlucky as often as they were lucky. They lived as if they had thousands of lives to spare, and in my father's stories, it seemed that they did.

If I had a thousand lives, I might have been more like my great-uncles: braver, bolder, and wilder. But I have only one life, at least only one at a time, and in this life, I am my father's daughter and my grandfather's granddaughter. Like them, I am the observer, the outsider, always in the middle of a story but never at the center of it.

Sometimes, I think I would like for someone else to tell a story about me. I would like for someone to imagine me the way I am always imagining other people: my great-grandfather who died of the loss of land, the stress caused by the loss, the sleepless nights. I imagine him standing at the edge of his small plot of land, in the dead of night, surrounded by fields and paddies that no longer belong to him. The blooming rice smells soft and sweet, a dog howls in the distance, and the water of the paddies glints silver in the moonlight. If my great-grandfather had been a woman, I think it would have been said that he died of a broken heart.

But no one will imagine me the way I imagine my great-grandfather because nothing has ever happened to me. Nothing as bad or as important or as final as death. My sufferings, though numerous, are small. They are so small that even all together, listed by magnitude, or in chronological order, I am afraid they will not have the weight to shift any balance, to change anything or anyone. This is the reason I am the storyteller and not the story. I do not have the makings of a protagonist. I do not like to make decisions, to take risks, to assert or involve myself. I have never hit another person, never punched, slapped, or even pushed. I do not want to touch what causes me aversion. I do not want to throw my body against it. I prefer to keep my body to myself, to keep myself to myself. I want someone else to imagine me at the center of a story because I believe if they got it right, if they told the right story about me, then I could live inside that story, inside someone else's words, and the words would create the person I wanted to be so I would not have to pretend to be that person anymore.

After the death of her husband and her eldest son, my great-grandmother gathered her surviving children around and asked them what they wished to become. A single word laden with longing and hope. And because the verbs are left un-conjugated in Burmese, left untouched, the same word describes the past, present, and future. What will they come to be, these fatherless children? Their mother was a landowner's wife, a landowner's widow, a woman who had never worked with her hands. All she had left now were the family jewels, like those my other great-grandmother, my mother's grandmother, sold, one by one, to educate her sons. My father's grandmother sold her jewels as well, and for the same purpose, though she had enough sense to ask her sons first if they wanted an education.

My grandfather was the only one to say yes. His elder brother chose to inherit what was left of the land, and his younger brothers were too little to know what they wanted.

I do not know what it was my great-grandmother wanted. Long ago, before the first baby, before her marriage. I do not know what she had wished to become when she was a child. Was it to be a landowner's wife? The wife of an anxious, fragile man. The kind of man who would die of heartbreak, not over the loss of a person, but over the loss of land. Had my great-grandmother wanted a daughter? Had she wanted children at all? *Whatever you wish to become,* my father said my great-grandmother told her sons, *I will work so you will become, I will make it happen.*

Nights when my great-grandfather walked the fields, trespassing on land that no longer belonged to him, hoping perhaps to be bitten by a poisonous snake, hoping perhaps to die and haunt the fields forever, I imagine my great-grandmother slept soundly in her bed under the canopy of a mosquito net, her long hair spread in a dark halo around her head. Her eyelids flutter like a moth against the light, and she is trapped inside a beautiful dream of a different life, a life where she had married a stronger man, or had married no one at all. A dream of running barefoot in the dirt, climbing trees, and bathing in the river; things my great-grandmother had perhaps never done, being a woman of a certain class, the mother of a formerly prosperous family. I imagine this dream for her anyway. The earth warm under her bare feet, her thick braid slapping against her back with each step, and her body weightless, flying like an arrow to its mark.

Denver

It was the city she had prayed for, had longed for the way women in fairy tales long for children. For nearly a year she had built the city with her own desire, for warmth, blue skies, belonging. Lying sleepless in her twin bed or kneeling before a statue of the Lady of Lourdes, she had made promises and begged without shame. It was a bit like falling in love.

She had never seen the city before, not even in photographs. She feared that photographs would replace the city she had built in her mind. No one she knew had spent much time in the city, though everyone spoke of it. Everyone spoke of every city because *city* itself was the magic word. They all longed to be where people were.

And when she finally arrived, it was not to the city of her desire, but an entirely different place. Flat and functional, its colors bleached by the perpetual sun. Her apartment was empty of furniture so the first thing she did was go to a mattress store to buy a mattress. The salesman asked for her name and she gave it to him, spelled out each letter slowly. One r and two i's at the end. M as in Mary, n as in Nancy. When she was finished, the man looked at what he had written down and it was correct. She felt relieved. But then he kept looking at her name. He looked up at her and asked, *Where does your name come from?*

Because she had woken early that morning to get to the airport, and because she had not eaten anything before her flight, she answered automatically, *My mother, she made it up.* She was too tired and too hungry to process the real question behind his question. I mean, the salesman said, *What is your ethnicity?* And again, she answered without thinking, as if stating her date of birth, her weight and height—*Burmese*, she said, even though it was not an ethnicity but a nationality, and one that no longer existed. *Oh*, the salesman said. He looked at her the same way he had been looking at her name. *Is it Burma or Myanmar?* he asked. Before she could answer, he began telling her what he knew about the coup and the dictatorship, which was very little.

In that moment, what she fixated on, what made her angry was the fact that he mispronounced Myanmar as Ma-yen-mar. *It's Myanmar*, she said.

She was afraid to speak to anyone in the city after that first encounter at the mattress store. She felt that what had happened with the salesman had been her fault. She must have signaled to him in some way that she was willing to answer his questions, that she was at his service. She remembered now that her mother was rarely kind to strangers in this country. Her mother rarely made eye contact, rarely smiled, and boldly ignored questions that were directed at her. It used to embarrass her, what she thought was her mother's rudeness.

She was beginning to understand her mother better now. She ate her meals on the floor in front of her coffee table because she did not want to buy more furniture. The coffee table was found at the back of a thrift store, the kind of place where the sole cashier is too tired to make small talk.

In the place where she lived before, the place that was not a city, she had longed to be with others. She had longed for crowds and noise. Now, in the city of sunshine and crisp mountain air, she did not like to leave her apartment. Once, two of her friends came to visit her in the city, and when she took them to a park, a man accosted them. A man she had never seen before, a stranger. The kind of man her mother had warned her about as a child. A lu sein, a green person, unripe, unknown. Because green was an unlucky color for her mother, a color her mother never wore, she understood that green people, strangers, were to be avoided as well. She and her friends were walking through the park when the man walked up beside them and smiled. She did not smile back. The man drew uncomfortably close. Her instinct was to put her body between him and the bodies of her friends. Then the man spoke. *Do you come from Vietnam?* he said, still smiling, his eyes darting between her and her female friend. *No*, she said, pushing the word at him. No, we do not come from Vietnam. No, we do not want to talk to you. For a second the man's smile lingered, the way a decapitated body continues to move even after its head is cut off. Then the smile slipped off his face and she walked away.

She walked and walked, but there was no place in the city where she could be alone. The ceaseless blue sky gave her no privacy, no space or separation from the heavens. She felt there was no distance left between the holy and herself and so the holy was no longer holy. It was obscenely green parks and unrelenting sunlight. Streets that ran in straight lines and met one another at perfect right angles. The highway to the mountains packed with cars every weekend.

There was no place in the city, she thought, where the Lady of Lourdes might appear. No grotto, cave, dell, or ravine, no shade for an apparition. She went for walks along the secluded trail behind her apartment building, passed chain-link fences, ditches, and alleyways, where on Wednesdays her neighbor's garbage cans would be lined up stinking. The trail ended at a park, adjacent to a looming hospital, and if she walked to the middle of it, past the golf course, but just before the community pool, she could almost pretend she was no longer in the city. The Lady of Lourdes appeared to a young girl in the countryside and for a long time the girl was not believed. If she had been the one to see the Lady, she would not have told anyone. She would have kept the Lady to herself, her own private miracle.

Another time, she was at a dive bar at the edge of the city. The bar was across the street from an art gallery where literary events were often held. Both the bar and the gallery were far from downtown and the surrounding gentrified or gentrifying areas were people who attended literary events usually drank. She did not drink, it was against the fifth precept, but she went to the bar anyway. As soon as she entered it, she knew she had made a mistake. Everyone inside stopped what they were doing and stared at the group she had entered with, stared at their relative wealth and privilege, their collective whiteness. She does not know if her companions even noticed. She felt ashamed for having entered the bar with them, for being one of them, for having become one of them, and then felt ashamed for being ashamed of her friends and colleagues. She separated herself from the group and was making her way to the bar to ask for a glass of water when a man approached her and introduced himself. He was an elderly man, very drunk, with swan-white hair. *You are an Indian,* he said. *I can tell. I am part Indian too, a half-breed. What kind of Indian are you?* She said she was not any kind of Indian, sorry, but it was loud in the bar and he could not hear what she said, or maybe he did not listen. He said, *I know you are an Indian. Let me guess. No,* she said, and shook her head. *Are you Cherokee?* he said. *No,* she said. *Are you Lakota? Are you Sioux?* She shook her head no, no. *No, I am sorry, so sorry. I know what you are,* the man said. And she did not want to take that knowledge away from him. An elderly man with white hair and a white beard, cheeks collapsed and wrinkled. He did not look white or Native or anything else to her, only old, and she thought it was beautiful how time made everyone look more or less the same, and she really was sorry that she could not be for this elderly man a person he could recognize.

And it wasn't only strangers, strange men, who were the problem, who were to blame, who were *just trying to connect*. People she knew at the university were also complicit. They raved to her about Burmese restaurants in cities she had never been to and would probably never visit. They left newspaper clippings about the Rohingya in her campus mailbox. They told her that they too were always being mistaken for Scandinavian or German. *No one thinks I look American either.* They told her they too could relate to the weight of accumulation, since every time they walked down the street, they were catcalled. *Every single time.*

She was frequently catcalled, too, but her hearing was bad so she could never make out what had been said, what words had been flung at her from the car window before the men sped off, laughing. She could never tell if it had been a sexual or a racial slur or both. It didn't seem to matter. The men drove away, or she walked past them, and the interaction was over.

It was much worse when the interaction didn't end, when she didn't know how to end it. Such as the time she went to the Christmas market downtown and stumbled upon the aromatherapy shop. The shopkeeper was a large man, barrel-chested, with a big voice. As she and her boyfriend approached his tent, she heard the shopkeeper explaining something very loudly to a woman. She began perusing the different essential oils and her boyfriend wandered off. She asked the shopkeeper if he had any special formulas and he brought out a few for her to try. She smelled the first one and recognized the scent of jasmine. Her favorite lotion as a teenager was a light purple concoction called Night Blooming Jasmine; she treasured it so much and used it so sparingly that it eventually expired and rotted. *You have a good nose*, the shopkeeper said, and she was pleased. Then he said, *Where are you from?* She said, *California.* He paused, then said, *I mean, what is your heritage?* She did not know why, but for once, she decided not to answer. It was her last day in Denver before she went home for winter break, to the two-bedroom walk-up that her parents owned, the first home they ever owned, just a mile from her old middle school, where her mother still worked. She said to the shopkeeper, *I'd rather not tell you.* He said, *OK.* Then he said, *You know, I only asked because jasmines don't grow in this country.* She said, *I told you I was from California.* He said, *But were you born there?* She said, *Do you ask your white customers that question?* He said, *Yes, I do.* She said, *I don't believe you.* He said, *I ask people where they come from all the time and you are the first person who reacted this way.* He said, *I don't know what you are ashamed of.* He said, *Denver is a melting pot.* He said, *My wife and I, we have traveled all over the world.* He then began listing all the countries they had been to, but she was angry and crying and could not speak. Her boyfriend, her future husband, found her and led her away. *Next time*, he said to the shopkeeper, *just say sorry.* The shopkeeper called after them in a singsong voice, *Sorry.*

Someone once told her all the trees in the city were planted by settlers, and even though she did not believe it, she began to feel a tenderness toward the trees. As she drove to the university through a tunnel of green, the trees on either side evenly spaced, all the same girth and height, it was easy for her to imagine them as saplings growing neatly in a row. The surrounding city not yet a city, but an open plain. The trees had been brought here by forces outside of their control, she thought, but unlike her, they could not leave, but had to continue growing in this strange land where no trees had grown before. It pained her to think that if the settlers had not planted the trees, had not received shade from the alpine sun, perhaps they would not have stayed, would not have colonized the land and violently displaced the natives. It pained her to think that it was the trees that had made this city livable for them, that made it desirable, even when there was no gold found in the river. The river was buried beneath the city now, enclosed on either bank by concrete walls that rose up to boulevards and streets. Only the city's most desolate inhabitants, the city's exiles, sought shelter at the water's edge, sleeping under the shade of a bridge when a tree could not be found.

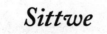

Sittwe

My mother, father, and elder sisters spent their last years in Burma, the years leading up to my birth, in Sittwe, the capital of Rakhine State. My parents were transferred there as part of what my father described as a well-intentioned, though ultimately failed, government initiative to send educated professionals to the most remote and underdeveloped regions of the country. The initiative was a failure because many people who were transferred simply did not go and those who went did not stay. My parents were among the few who accepted their assignment, and who stayed for the full three years of their term.

When I asked my mother why they decided to go, she said, *I can't even remember now*. Then, she repeated in English, *I don't know why we made that decision*. Even after living in America for over a quarter of a century, my mother still pronounced certain words in a vaguely British way. The t's in her *don't* and *that* were crisp, precise. I always had the impression that my mother's Bamar was sloping and rushed, while her English, learned from Anglican nuns, stood up very straight and proper. *We didn't want to be cowards*, my mother said, switching back to Bamar. *We didn't want to be so selfish. Maybe we felt we had a debt to repay. A duty to our country. I don't know*, she said.

When I was a child, before I knew where or what exactly Sittwe was, I knew that it was a place of exile. For as long as I could remember, my family had lived in places where we did not belong, where people asked us where we came from—but my mother and father never spoke of the places where we lived, where I grew up, as places of exile. Sittwe alone was exilic. *It was like falling into an abyss*, my mother always said. The word she used, meaning gorge, pit, or chasm, rhymed with the word meaning fear. Like falling into fear, I heard.

My parents received their transfer orders in December of 1986, five months after my middle sister was born. At the time, my father was teaching at RC3, Regional College Three, a two-year college that had been established, as if miraculously, right before my father graduated from university with what he had thought would be a useless degree in English. My mother, who had graduated with a degree in education, was teaching at my parents' alma mater, RASU, Rangoon Arts and Sciences, formerly named Rangoon University.

It was an iconic university, the birthplace of every nationwide anti-colonial strike, and of numerous anti-government protests. Famously, when the UN secretary-general U Thant passed away and the government refused him a state burial, students from the university kidnapped U Thant's body and erected a makeshift tomb for him on campus. I was told this story when I visited the university the summer between my sophomore and junior years of college when I returned to Burma. By then, it was renamed University of Yangon. The campus was beautiful and decrepit, every stone facade stained with what looked like rain, but was likely mold, the peeling paint of the walls a light hospital green, and the stairs crumbling. My mother showed me her old office and classrooms, but also the places on campus where student protestors had been shot and killed, by the police, by the military. None of these places were marked with plaques or statues. When I asked questions too loudly, my mother told me to keep my voice down.

Sittwe is located on an estuarial island along the eastern coast of the Bay of Bengal. *A kyun*, my mother always said, drawing out the word. Kyun. Island. In English, the two-syllable word is paradisal; an island is a place of escape, of wonder, land appearing where land was not expected. In Bamar, the one-syllable kyun, with its elongated vowel, is dismal, claustrophobic; a kyun is a place trapped by water, a forsaken place, a place of banishment. By consonance it evokes the word for narrow, kyin, and the word for tight, kyat. *Sittwe was a kyun*, my mother always said, when I asked her what the city was like. An estuarial island, surrounded not only by the ocean, but by rivers as well, vulnerable to both cyclones and floods.

My father was appointed the English department chair and my mother a tutor at Sittwe Degree College. The college had recently transitioned from being a two-year institution to a four-year institution and my father was sent to build up the English department. It was technically a promotion for him, since in Rangoon, at RC3, he had been a tutor like my mother. My parents fought over how I should represent their official titles. *Say "lecturer,"* my father said. *You weren't a lecturer yet at RC3*, my mother said. *If she says "tutor,"* my father said, *people here won't know what she means.*

People here or *people from here* was a phrase my father used often. My father was always reminding my mother of the limitations of the *people here*, of the importance of translating for them, of making oneself intelligible to them. Growing up, I picked up from context that *people here* were largely ignorant, though not necessarily unkind. They were capable of acting fairly and even generously, but only if steered in the right direction. My father never asked anything of *people here*. If they could not understand or accept that a word could have different meanings in different places to different people, he simply changed the word. *Say "lecturer,"* my father said. *People here don't think of tutors as teachers and that's what we were.* The word for teacher in Bamar was *saya* for men and *sayama* for women, titles of respect. *We were teachers*, my father said firmly, *saya sayama*.

Before the move to Sittwe, my mother had never really left home. She was born in Rangoon, and with the exception of some childhood years spent in Katha and Moulmein, she had never left the capital. Katha was in the north, in Sagaing, bordering Kachin State, and Moulmein was in Mon State, bordering Tanintharyi, the long, narrow region of the country that resembled the tail of a kite. My mother's father was an income tax officer and had been transferred to both places in his time. On a map, Katha and Moulmein seemed as distant from Rangoon as Sittwe was, but in reality, they were much closer. At that time, Sittwe was accessible only by air or by sea. There was no land route yet through the Rakhine Yoma, the mountain range that isolated Rakhine State from the rest of the country.

My mother knew little about Sittwe and about Rakhine State, but she had heard the name of the river that ran through the state and the city. *Kispanadi,* my mother said, savoring the four syllables. *I thought it was so romantic,* she said, *such a beautiful name.* My mother held on to that name like it was a promise.

When the family arrived in Sittwe, however, they were greeted by the black waters of the Kispanadi River, and eternally gloomy skies. The apartment they had been promised was not yet available and they had to stay in a hotel until the previous tenants moved out. The hotel was expensive and my parents had to pay for it themselves. Even decades later, my mother was still angry about this. *Why didn't they say they weren't ready for us?* my mother asked. *Why didn't they say, "please don't come yet"?* Then, she answered her own questions. *They were afraid we wouldn't come,* she said, *they were afraid that if they delayed, we would change our minds.*

The long-awaited apartment was a two-bedroom in a government-owned building. The larger of the bedrooms was haunted, so the whole family slept together in the smaller one. The apartment had a kitchen, a living room, and a bathroom. Standard government housing, though luxurious by local standards. The building was full of lu gyi, my mother said, big people, high-ranking officials from various departments and ministries. *Everyone thought it was a wonderful place to live,* my mother said, *but we were so unhappy.* The electricity came on only between six in the evening and midnight. Running water was available only between five and six in the morning. My father said their apartment building received more water than others in the city because the engineer in charge of the city's plumbing lived there. He made sure the water in the building ran for the full hour.

I have never been to Sittwe, but all my life I believed I was conceived there. I imagined it had happened in the haunted room, since the children, my sisters, went to sleep early in the smaller bedroom, which the whole family shared.

Later, I learned that my parents were back in Rangoon when I was conceived. My mother had returned in March of 1988 when the government closed colleges and universities in response to protests over the death of a student at RIT, Rangoon Institute of Technology, who was shot and killed by riot police. My parents referred to the widespread protests as the *Phone Maw ayekhin*. Ko Phone Maw was the name of the student who was killed, and ayekhin meant demonstrations, marches. Most often I have seen it translated as uprising. It is a word whose power has no equivalent for me in English. A word that has the word ye, write, inside of it. An ayekhin was an effort to write history, with one's body, with one's life.

My parents knew the larger bedroom in Sittwe was haunted because the first night they tried to sleep there, my mother, my father, my two-year-old eldest sister, and my five-month-old middle sister, no one could get any rest. The children were pulled awake by invisible hands. A ghostly figure was sighted in their mosquito net. *We were haunted the whole night*, my mother said, *we couldn't sleep at all.*

A condition of ghostliness is restlessness, which is why people who stay out too late are called street ghosts or street haunters. Later, my mother learned that someone had died in the room. In their apartment building, many people died, from sickness, old age, or natural disasters. A neighbor, an older unmarried woman who befriended my mother, said the tenants in their building died in fours, dropping off one after the other until every seat at a dining table was filled. In death, just as in life, people did not like to eat alone. Ghosts, too, longed for company. Hearing the story about the haunted bedroom, I wondered if I was the ghost who haunted my family, if I was the presence that had kept them awake with my demand to be felt and seen, to be a part of the family.

II

Leymyethna

My great-grandfather was reborn in a woman's body, in my body, my mother said, because he had been a vain, arrogant, and comfort-seeking man. He died of a blood vessel that ruptured in his brain. In Bamar, to have a stroke is to have wind cut off. Cut, severed, or crossed over, as when my great-grandfather crossed over to death, or when my family crossed over to Thailand and then the United States, and never returned. Strokes are caused by high blood pressure and high blood pressure is caused, in part, by stress. In moments of stress, people cut themselves off, or are cut off, from a family, a culture, a nation, even from a life.

My great-grandfather felt dizzy and asked for the doctor. Then he sat down in his chair and died. He died right away, my grandmother told my mother, he did not suffer much. My great-uncle, the eldest son, never called the doctor, or he delayed, or he called the doctor only after his father had died. This great-uncle was the one who was later sent to Rangoon for an education, the one for whom royal jewels were sold. He was sent away even before he had graduated from secondary school. Despite all my great-grandmother's efforts, he did not graduate.

Many years after the end of the war, and the end of my great-grandfather's life, I went to the Colorado School of Traditional Chinese Medicine and asked the students there to tell me what was wrong with me. The first time I asked, they said they would consult their supervisor. The second time I asked, at the end of my appointment when I was already checking out at the front desk, the student behind the desk told me my diagnosis: blood deficiency with internal wind. *What does that mean?* I asked, and the student seemed reluctant to explain. *It has to do with your blood circulation*, she said, *and wind can be related to strokes, paralysis, seizures, anything like that.*

I did not tell the student that I was reincarnated from my great-grandfather or that he had died of a hemorrhagic stroke, because even at a traditional Chinese medicine clinic, I suspected that this information would seem irrelevant. I thanked the student and made an appointment to see her again the next week.

The war came to an end soon after my great-grandfather's death. Bombs stopped falling on cities and the family was able to come out of hiding and return home. Home was a house in the city of Hinthada, a port city by the Irrawaddy River, where my great-grandfather and great-grandmother had settled after their marriage. I do not know why my great-grandmother did not stay in the village of Leymyethna, her ancestral home. I do not know why she chose to leave her parents' house, for the first time as a bride, and the second time as a widow. I do not know why but I know that she did: she returned to Hinthada with her seven children and a trunk full of jewels. She would not leave the city again. Forty years after my great-grandfather's death, my great-grandmother would die in the city, in Hinthada, in the house that had withstood the British bombs and Japanese bombs.

And it was a miracle their house had withstood the bombs and the looters. Many of their neighbors' homes had been destroyed. Some of their neighbors never returned. Every night, my great-grandmother walked through the house casting prayers of protection so the family would not be robbed, so the jewels her late husband had inherited would be safe in the attic where she hid them.

When my great-grandfather was still alive, he kept the family jewels locked in a chest, a chest he would habitually open with a key, so he could gaze upon his mother's treasure. Even then, long before the jewels were sold, one by one, they were already relics of a lost time, of a slaughtered and exiled monarchy. My great-grandfather's mother was a princess, a niece of the last true king. The very last king of Burma was not a true king, my mother always said. He came into power only because his mother-in-law had all of his brothers and sisters put to death, all the princes and princesses with a claim to the throne. It was bad luck to spill royal blood upon the earth, so the princesses were strangled, and the princes were thrown into sacks and beaten to death. In other stories, they were rolled into carpets and trampled by elephants. My great-grandfather's mother only escaped because she was not a daughter of the king. She was a daughter of the king's elder brother. She escaped from the palace with her life and the jewels she was wearing on her body.

I find a detailed fact sheet on my diagnosis of blood deficiency: Some Causes, Potential Signs, What to Do.

Causes: eating poorly, thinking too much
Signs: dry skin, hair loss, numbness, dizziness, poor memory, difficulty focusing, depression, anxiety, stress, difficulty falling asleep, a feeling of disembodiment, lack of strength, headaches and migraines
To Do: everything I have already tried

I wondered if my great-grandfather exhibited the same potential signs before he died. If he too had tried meditation, yoga, chi kung, cooking, reading, and walking. I wondered if he too had had seizures. The tingling in his hands and feet, the hazy feeling, like a curtain drawn over the whole world, and then the tightening, the loss of control, his body wrung out and warped. Did he feel the shame of being conscious through it all? Through the interminable seconds that it lasted? Did he try to hide the seizures the way I did, for years and from everyone around him? Did he live in fear of his own body, of not knowing when or how it would betray him, of not knowing why?

When I was younger, my mother and father feared I would grow up to be too much like my great-grandfather. I was their youngest and most American child, and they feared that the vices of the aristocracy would resurface in my relatively privileged person: laziness, indulgence, arrogance. *Don't be such a smart-ass*, my father said to me one morning when we were stopped in traffic. I cannot remember what I had been saying. It was the only time my father ever swore at me.

My mother said my pride was too quick to swell, and I had to learn to suppress it. She wanted me to be gentle and sweet. Hearing those words, I wanted nothing more than to break them with my hands. I wanted nothing more than to kill. I believed, at times, that I was capable of murder. Not the murder of a living being, for that was against the first precept, but the murder of a living idea, a concept: gentleness, sweetness, femininity. I did not understand why my parents were so intent on reforming me when I had already been born into a woman's body. I did not know what I had left to lose in the next life.

My great-grandfather was a beautiful man, my mother said my grandmother told her. He had fine, intelligent eyes, dark eyebrows, and a noble bearing. He also had lavish tastes. He enjoyed rich foods, silken fabrics, leather-bound books. I do not know if he had a library, but I imagine if he did, it would be filled with only heavy, dark volumes. My great-grandfather was an educated man. He went to a university in Sri Lanka, back when it was called Ceylon. He studied agriculture. He was a gentleman-farmer, a landowner who lived in a city, in Hinthada, a city large enough to be bombed during the war. My great-grandfather spoke English when he studied in Ceylon. His tongue formed the same words I form now, his hands as he held the fountain pen, his eyes as they moved across a page. I wonder if he resisted the language in the privacy of his mind, in the realm of his dreams. I wonder if he knew he would succumb to it one day, in a future life, in a body no longer his own.

I once rushed to the mirror when I felt one of my seizures coming on. The familiar tightening in my feet, the familiar dread. The mirror I sought was the floor-to-ceiling one that covered the sliding doors of the closet I shared with my sisters, a mirror that covered an entire wall of our bedroom, that reflected everything in that room back to us. I knelt by the mirror because I wanted to see what I was not supposed to see, Medusa's face, the Gorgon's head, my own face turned to stone. I wanted to see what I looked like when I was no longer myself, no longer in control of my face or my body. It was like a view into my past lives, or my future lives, a view I should not have had. When chanting the metta sutta, the discourse of loving-kindness, one sends metta to both beings that are good to be seen with the eyes and beings that are not good to be seen with the eyes. As a child, I asked my mother who the latter beings were, and she said ghosts, spirits, and devas, which she translated as angels, were all beings who were not easy to see. She did not say they could not be seen because she herself saw them sometimes. Not good to be seen did not mean invisible. It only meant difficult to see, difficult to look at. It was difficult to look at myself in the mirror as my face tightened, hardened, and changed. I wanted to be pretty, I wanted to be beautiful, and it was terrible, terrible to see what I was instead. A ghost, a spirit, or an angel. Not good to be seen with the eyes. I looked anyway. I fixed my gaze on the mirror as best I could and looked and looked at what it had to show me. I kept looking long after the episode had passed, long after I was myself again.

Yangon

The first time I returned to the city where I was born, my little cousin swung a metal pipe in the front yard of our grandparents' house, and it hit my eldest sister, and she bled, and cried, and believed she would be poisoned by the rust. That night, and every night after that, during our short visit, she had terrible, fevered dreams, dreams that infected me and my middle sister since we slept beside her beneath the same mosquito net. Collectively, we dreamed of the crawl space underneath the house, the darkness there, red screams, and the glint of metal. My mother said the house was cursed. The house where she grew up, on a tree-lined street with a wrought iron gate and jasmines blooming in the garden. The house where she lived with her father and mother even after she was married, even after she had given birth to her first child. The house where my brother had fallen ill. The house he never returned to. My eldest sister believed the house was trying to kill her a second time; she begged my mother to never bring her back there again.

My eldest sister has not returned to Yangon since. My middle sister has returned three times. My middle sister was once my great-grandmother, my wife in our past life. My mother says I followed her into this life. Before my middle sister was conceived, my great-grandmother appeared to my mother in a dream, her long white hair loose down her back, a thin gown covering her nakedness. My great-grandmother told my mother she was coming to her, coming to take refuge in my mother's body. My mother panicked. She had plans to go back to school, a scholarship to pursue her master's in England. My mother begged her grandmother to come back another time, she made promises, tried to compromise. But my great-grandmother said there would be no other time. This was her only chance. When my mother awoke from the dream, she cried, and my father comforted her, reminding her that they had been careful, that there was no chance she was pregnant.

A few weeks later, my mother found out that she was.

The second time I returned to Yangon, I arrived four days before my twentieth birthday, and ten days before my twenty-first. The first birthday was measured by the Gregorian calendar, and the second by the Burmese. I had two birthdays every year: June 9, and whatever date fell six days after the new moon of Nayon, the third month of the Burmese year, corresponding with Gemini, the third sign of the zodiac. By the Burmese measurement of age, a person was as old as the year in which she lived, and not the year she had completed. Age was measured by the present, not the past.

My mother always said I must have been reborn from one of the student protestors in the 8888 strike, because I was born ten months after the uprising and nine months after the bloody coup that followed. My mother did not like to imagine that I had suffered a violent death, but I romanticized the uprising and the young people who had died for it—shot down in the streets, suffocated in a police van, or executed in the prison yard. I liked to believe this was the brief life I had had, between my great-grandfather's and mine, the life of an activist, a revolutionary, a martyr.

That summer I turned twenty in Yangon, my mother showed me the clinic at the edge of the city where I was born, and where my elder sisters were born before me. She pointed out the building from a distance. I looked out the car window. The building was dark and boxy, provincial. My mother said the clinic had been small and run-down even twenty, twenty-five years ago when we were born. The children's hospital in the city center was modern and impressive, but my mother was afraid to return there. It was the place where my brother was born, and the place where he had died.

Earlier or later, our relatives took us to the artificial lake in the center of the city, the lake where my mother and father had been married in a palatial hall on a copy of a royal barge. The barge was called Karaweik, in the singular, though there were two mythical birds shouldering the weight of the hall. We walked out onto the docks, my mother and I, and posed for many pictures with Karaweik and the Shwedagon Pagoda in the background. All around us, young couples were embracing by the water, hidden among the trees, and though I knew that my brother had died at the children's hospital, I also believed he had drowned in the lake. The great royal lake in the center of the city that was constructed by the British. It was an artificial lake fed by pipes that diverted water from an artificial reservoir.

I think it made my mother sad to return to the place where she had married my father without my father. Yangon, or Rangoon, as my parents still called it, belonged to both of them. It was the city where they grew up, where they met, and where they fell in love. My mother and father were both nineteen years old when they fell in love, and younger when they met. My father wooed my mother by borrowing her books and returning them with love letters tucked inside. That is the story I have always been told. Maybe it was just one borrowed book, just one letter, but in my mind, that single letter multiplied and reproduced, and I imagine my young mother opening book after book and discovering love letter after love letter. My young mother, nineteen, or perhaps still eighteen years old when she receives the first letter, when the first book is returned. The girl who would one day become my mother, but who is yet a stranger to me. I see her always in the moment of opening a book, the moment of my conception, I think, a moment that begins interminably, begins over and over again, so the book in my mother's hands is always the first one, and the love letter she finds always still unopened.

My parents had attended the same high school, English Methodist, and the same university, Rangoon Arts and Sciences. Their high school was so large that they did not meet until after they graduated, at a party thrown for students from their school who were going to the same university. My mother and father were introduced at this party. For the rest of the summer, my mother said, she kept seeing my father everywhere around the city: at the market, on the bus, at the cinema. When the rains came and my parents started at the university, my mother became friends with my father's cousin, a second or third cousin, and my father used this connection between them to borrow my mother's books and return them with love letters hidden inside. My mother read the love letters and wrote her own in return. They began to date. This meant they ate lunch together and rode the city bus home together. After dating for five years, they were pressured by my father's parents, who were planning to move to the United States, to get married. They did. It was April 1982. They were both twenty-four years old.

Exactly a year later, my mother and father will have birthed and lost a child, my elder brother. For the rest of their lives, my mother will speak of my brother incessantly and my father will hardly speak of him at all.

What my mother will say: that he was such a handsome, chubby baby. Fair skin, clear brown eyes, black velvety hair. A perfect, healthy baby boy. Seven pounds, two ounces. Born in Tabaung, March, the last month of the Burmese year, the beginning of summer. A Wednesday son, like his grandfather, my mother's father. They brought him home to my mother's parents' house, where my mother and father lived after they were married. They were so happy, my mother and father. Two newlyweds, new parents. Their happiness lasted several days, maybe a week, maybe longer. Then, my brother fell ill. He would not drink milk. Or, he would drink and then vomit, become dehydrated. They took him back to the children's hospital where he was born. Then they brought him home. He did not get better. They took him to the hospital again, and this time, they had to leave him there.

What my father will not say: if he had wanted a boy, a son. If he ever felt disappointment that the next three children were all girls, all daughters, though we called ourselves by the pronoun tha, son, instead of thamee, daughter. If he ever blamed himself for my brother's death, for not being in the delivery room when my brother was born, when the medical student pulled him out of my mother's body with forceps. If his aversion to hospitals and doctors began with my brother's stay in the neonatal intensive care unit. If he had always been anxious and protective, cautious to a fault, or if there was a time before my brother's death when he had been more care-free, more trusting. If there was a time when he believed that nothing bad could ever happen to him or to anyone he loved.

Minbu

Many miles up the Irrawaddy River from my grandfather's small village of Gayan, past Rangoon, which sprawled farther in the east, past Hinthada, which was cradled in the river's bend, so far north that Sittwe lay on the other side of the Rakhine Yoma, my grandmother was born in the small city of Minbu, on the western bank of the Irrawaddy.

My grandmother was her parents' only child, but she was not their firstborn. There had been three other babies born before her who died in infancy. All three had been sons. My grandmother, like me, was the fourth-born child, the first to live, while I was the third. My father said my grandmother said when she was born, her father did not come home for a week. For a full week, he stayed away because he could not bear to see her, could not bear to meet yet another child he might lose. At the end of the week, however, when my great-grandfather finally came home, when he looked upon my grandmother for the first time, he fell in love.

I never liked the number four, never thought of myself as the fourth child in my family. Three was my favorite number. Three, which sounded like my name and had its shape when written down. *T*, *h*, and *r* were the three consonants with which I identified. I thought *four*, *ley*, which in Bamar was a homonym for heavy, also sounded heavy in English. Four like *door* or *oar*, the immense weight of water. Four was a masculine number, I thought, like all even numbers. In Bamar numerals, it was the mirror image of three. A number that is replicated from three, though darkly, since all mirrors are to be wary of, all mirrors reflect the world slightly askew, revealing ghosts who cannot be seen with the naked eye, or not revealing the living dead who have no reflection. In Bamar, four is the first number that is reflected, the beginning of the descent into reproduction. Like my grandmother, I am the fourth-born child, but graciously, my brother died so I could become the third in my family, the third of three daughters. Three is the most common number in fairy tales.

My grandmother's father fell in love with her, my father said, and did not want another child. Once afraid to love my grandmother at all, my great-grandfather became afraid of un-loving her should another child be born, perhaps a younger brother, a son. *He did not want his daughter to have to share his love with anyone*, my father said. But my great-grandmother had to share her husband's love. My great-grandfather had affairs, and eventually a mistress. This was the other reason they did not have more children after my grandmother. My father said my great-grandfather's affairs began when they lost their firstborn sons. *That was his excuse*, my father said. My grandmother was the last fruit of her parents' love, of whatever love still remained after the deaths that came between them.

My great-grandparents met and fell in love in Rangoon, just as my parents would two generations later. Like my parents, who were introduced by my father's cousin, my great-grandparents were also introduced by a family member, my great-grandmother's older sister. My great-grandfather, who was studying law at university, was a boarder at my great-grandmother's sister's neighbor's house. He met my great-grandmother when she came to Rangoon, to stay with her sister.

Back in her village, my great-grandmother was receiving many offers of marriage, and her father was eager for her to accept one of them. My great-grandmother and her older sister were children from their father's first marriage, and their father, who had recently remarried a younger woman, was anxious to have his grown daughter leave the house. He was ready to marry my great-grandmother off to anyone, my father said my grandmother said, even to the neighboring village chief's son, who had come to court my great-grandmother dressed in a paso, a garment better known by the Malay word sarong, and close-toed leather shoes. My great-grandmother tried not to laugh, my father said my grandmother said. *Nobody wore shoes in Burma*, my father explained, *especially not in the jungle, and especially not with a paso.*

My great-grandmother's older sister invited her to come to Rangoon to save her from their father and from her country suitors. My great-grandfather, an educated man from a well-to-do family, was considered to be a far superior match. I assume he also wore hnyat phanat, sandals, like a sensible person and a proud nationalist.

Despite his infidelity, my father said my great-grandfather had many good qualities. Among them were his humility, his sense of humor, and his kindness. To illustrate my great-grandfather's character, my father shared two stories.

The first story had to do with my great-grandfather's older brother, who was also his neighbor in Minbu. My great-grandfather's older brother was an official in the British colonial government, and thought so highly of himself that he had his servants call him "paya," or "lord," which, historically, was a form of address reserved for royalty. As a prank, my great-grandfather paid the neighborhood children to address him as "paya" as well. I do not know how long this went on, but eventually, my great-grandfather's older brother found out, and was so furious he showed up at my great-grandfather's house brandishing a government-issued gun.

In the second story, a drunk man was loitering outside my great-grandparents' house, raging and cursing. When the curses became personal, my great-grandfather went outside to confront the man. This ended with him punching the man in the face. Once on the ground, however, the drunk man began to cry, and my great-grandfather felt so bad, so sorry, he ended up giving the man a small fortune.

The next day, and for many days after, all the drunks in Minbu gathered outside my great-grandparents' house, walking in circles, hoping to be punched.

Of my great-grandmother, my father said she was a soft person, pyau, which also meant weak or passive. My father said my great-grandmother was never angry about my great-grandfather's affairs. She was the kind of person who could not feel anger at all, he said.

Once, my great-grandfather's sisters found the address of a woman who was having an affair with their brother, and they brought my great-grandmother to this woman's doorstep to confront her. When the woman opened the door, my great-grandmother's sisters-in-law began berating her, and like the drunk in the other story, the woman began to cry. Instead of joining her sisters-in-law, my great-grandmother pulled them away from the woman's house, and begged them to never do something like that again.

I do not know how my father extracted all these stories about his grandparents from my grandmother when I could never get her to tell me anything about her life. Before my grandmother passed away, and before her dementia, I had tried many times to ask her about her youth, her childhood. She was the only grandparent whom I saw regularly growing up, and whom I continued to see, twice a year, whenever I went home. My father's father passed away a couple of years after I met him for the first time, when I was still a child, my mother's mother passed away even earlier, and my father's father lived in Yangon, and I had only ever met him three times in my life.

My grandmother lived within walking distance from my parents, and I saw her weekly. When I was very young, my parents used to drop me off at my grandmother's house when they needed a babysitter. I remember my grandmother always offered me English biscuits out of a tin can, and I always refused. She would watch soap operas or beauty pageants she had taped, and I would sit by the window in the front room and watch the cars pass on Rainbow Drive, waiting for my parents' tiny white car to come into view. As a child, I never asked my grandmother any questions and the only question she ever asked me was *Would you like something to eat?* It was only after I left home, and only after my grandmother's health began to deteriorate, that I thought to ask her about her life. By then, it was too late. I never asked the right questions and I could never get my grandmother to talk. Everything I knew about her, I learned from my father.

It was from my father that I learned that my grandmother had had a golden childhood. My great-grandfather was a very successful lawyer, a defense attorney, maybe the most sought-after one in all of Minbu, and my grandmother grew up in a house so large it covered an entire block. As an only child, her father's beloved child, she was spoiled in exceptional ways. Once, my father said, my grandmother accidentally broke a drinking glass. Being rich people, my father said, even the glasses they used to drink water were expensive, and the one my grandmother broke had been imported from England. My grandmother's mother scolded her for her clumsiness, but her father brought her into the dining room, where the family's most valuable and precious china was on display in a glass cabinet. Porcelain plates, crystal goblets, decorative items, gifts from clients. My great-grandfather arranged all of it on the dining table. He then handed my grandmother a bat and instructed her to smash it all.

South Bend

Her first year, she ran around the lakes, Saint Joseph and Saint Mary. Saint Joseph was the smaller lake and Saint Mary the larger. They separated the university from the seminary and the women's college. Young priests and young women, the two groups that needed most to be sequestered. She began running around the lakes when the trees were green and stopped when they were bare, when it was so cold she could no longer feel her gloved hands. When the chipmunks disappeared, when the swans flew away. When it began to snow, and the snow melted and froze, and more snow fell over the ice.

Her mother called the city a taw myot when they first arrived. Her father had insisted on helping her move in and her mother had insisted on helping her father. She felt a bit embarrassed to have both her parents accompany her at the start of graduate school. It made her feel like she was back in the fifth grade and her father was waiting right outside the door of her classroom, ready to carry her backpack and charm her teacher. She was old enough to carry her own backpack, she thought, to move by herself. She had, after all, just returned from a year of living abroad, of speaking a foreign language, of traveling alone all over Europe.

A taw myot was what her mother called any place that was not a major city, not Yangon, not Bangkok. The way her mother said the word taw, wistfully, with a touch of pity, always evoked for her clashing emotions, pride and shame, longing and revulsion. Taw meant jungle, forest, wood, it meant rural, it meant wild. Because her mother was born in Yangon, the capital, and her father was born in Hmawbi, a rural township northwest of the city, her mother used to call her father a taw tha, a son of the taw, when she wanted to tease him for his simplicity. From the back seat of their rented car, she looked out at the flat horizon, the low trees, the low sky, the wide expanse of green on either side of Douglas Road. Taw myot was close, she thought, but not quite right. She was not yet familiar with the term rust belt.

She was on a special scholarship for people historically under-represented in higher education. This was the language the university used. First generation, low income, African American, Asian American, Hawaiian/Pacific Islander, Hispanic, Native American, and/or. She had not even applied for the scholarship, though she must have checked some boxes on her application or submitted a FAFSA, which automatically brought her under consideration. She chose to attend because of the scholarship and because the English department had allowed her to defer her admission when she received the fellowship to Spain. If she had had more ambition, or more money to pay for another round of application fees, maybe she would have reapplied, to more prestigious schools in more exciting cities. But she was like her father, a taw tha, with simple needs and desires. A stipend that paid for food and rent. A library. Some place to run or walk. She made a total of $10,000 a year. Her student loans from college amounted to three times that much. Still, she considered herself very lucky.

She began dating them perhaps because they were also broke, more broke than her, though equally uncomplaining. They reminded her of her uncle, the one who passed away from liver failure when she was in college, who smelled like leather and cigarettes, who always said *Don't do as I do, do as I say*. Like her uncle, they had close-cropped hair and aquiline features. Like her uncle, they were an affectionate drunk, not a belligerent one. Alcohol made them sentimental, it made them tell her how pretty she was, how much she meant to them, how lucky they were. Things no boy had ever said to her. The first night, they did not kiss, only cuddled on their couch, watching a classic science-fiction film. After they drove her back to her graduate-student housing, she had lain awake in her twin bed with a giant, crushing feeling of dread. Something had been set in motion, a choice had been made, and the dread arose perhaps from the knowledge that she was powerless to unmake it now, to stop or pause or turn back, she had to live out this choice, let it run its course.

For the next two years, she was glad she was not alone, through the cold, interminable winters, the snow falling steadily from November to May. She did not have a car and they drove her everywhere, to the grocery store, to restaurants, to parties at friends' apartments. Once, they even drove her to Lake Michigan, in the dead of winter, when all the gift shops were closed, and there was not a tourist in sight. She had never seen snow on a beach before. It looked unreal, the black water, the white snow, the icy sand. She got out of the car with the intention of walking down to the water. The wind felt like it was made of needles. She got back in the car.

By the time the snow from the first winter melted for good, she had moved away from the lakes and closer to the river. From her little blue house with its fenced-in yard, she ran down to the river, past Saint Joseph High School, its football field and stadium lights, past the old-age home and the preschool. She ran along on the East Bank Trail, through downtown South Bend, past the park by the dam and the fish ladders, the orange sculpture, under the tunnel, past the second park, under the bridge. When she finally stopped to walk, under the concrete bridge, with its vaguely patriotic graffiti, her body felt so hollow, so empty and light, that she would always feel the need to cry, to produce something from her body, a liquid or a sound. The trees and the grass and the water sharpened into focus, deepened in color, but she could never cry, never give back to the river, she could only begin running again.

She and three of her friends moved into the little blue house to-gether because its prior inhabitants had always thrown parties at the house and invited them. Every other party they went to took place in someone's spacious, brand-new, and utterly characterless apartment, every apartment exactly the same, same stairs, hallway, balcony, and duck pond. Only the blue house was unique. It was cramped and old, and every party there ended with people sitting or lying down on the drab kitchen floor.

Her room was the smallest one in the house, at the foot of the stairs, added on after a fire burned down the kitchen. It was built like a covered porch or a sunroom, except in a city with no sun. Her room got so cold in the winter she had to sleep with a space heater on through the night, afraid it would catch on fire. She did not know if anyone had died in the kitchen fire and did not want to find out.

She did not mind having the smallest room because she spent so much time in their apartment, anyway. Whole days, whole weekends, doing what, she cannot even remember now. Probably reading, watching movies, talking. There was not much else to do. They were from a truck-stop city in the south and used to this boredom. They watched football and basketball. They played video games. They listened to queer electropop and Atlanta rap. They had a tattoo of a character from the cover of a pulp science-fiction novel she had not read, had never even heard of.

They had already been dating for a few weeks when the subject of her race first came up. She had been telling them about the time an elderly man in front of the library asked her if she came from China. She had been sitting on the lawn with her friend's dog when this man and his wife and their dog approached. First, the man asked if her friend's dog came from China. The question struck her as ridiculous. *Her coat is so black and shiny*, the man said, *like your hair*. That was when he directed the question at her. *Do you come from China?*

They expressed the appropriate amusement and outrage at her story, but then fell silent. *But what is your ethnicity?* they asked shyly. Somehow, she felt proud that they had not even known. It seemed to prove to her that they did not have a fetish, that they liked her for who she was.

After the elderly man in front of the library, no one else in South Bend ever asked where she came from. No one on Notre Dame's campus, no one downtown, no one at the community learning center or the juvenile detention center where she volunteered. This did not mean there were no other incidents. Once, an undergraduate in a writing group she helped to facilitate mistook her for another student in the group who was Asian. Once, a man at a party kept joking she was married to her roommate because her roommate was South Asian American. Once, a classmate at a party at her house joked that she could not speak English when she did not hear his drink order. Once, at a job interview, the person interviewing her expressed surprise that she was recommended for the position of Spanish translator.

Despite the interviewer's doubts, she got the job. She worked for a psychology lab at the medical school that was studying the effects of racism on depression among Mexican American teenagers in South Bend. A colleague translated the surveys and consent forms from English to Spanish and she translated them back into English. The two versions, the original and her translation, were then compared. Months later, when the study was over, the principal investigator wrote to her with the results. Teenagers who had a sense of community were less prone to depression, even if they experienced the same levels of racism. Her problem, she realized then, was that she had no community, and had never had one, outside of her own nuclear family.

Her mother had warned her that she should never be with a person who was also born on a Friday. Two Friday borns, two hamsters, could not survive together. One or both of them had to die. She does not know who it would have been, her or them, but she believes her mother. Nights when they huddled together, separated from the snow, wind, and ice by only a thin sheet of glass, broken venetian blinds, she had felt, inexplicably, that they could not adequately protect each other. She remembers one night distinctly. They broke up over the course of nearly a year, but she remembers the first night, the first night the breakup felt real, inevitable. Lying in bed next to each other, after a disastrous fight, the kind where they had yelled and she had yelled and they both had cried all over the apartment before ending up in bed, exhausted, she had said, *I feel like a limb is being cut off.* And that was what it felt like, like the removal of a part of her body, a part of herself.

Later, when she was just beginning to date her husband, whom she knew, even then, she would one day marry—there had been no dread, no fear after their first kiss—she met a woman whose ex-girlfriend had gone on to have a baby with a man. The woman thought it was unfair, how her ex-girlfriend could now have an easy, so-called normal life. She suspected that this woman thought she too had gotten off easy, ending up with a man while her ex had become more openly queer. She thought the woman was probably right, but she did not really believe in fairness anymore.

Sittwe

My mother was so homesick in Sittwe that she flew back to Rangoon twenty-two times during the three years of her term. The first time she returned was in January of 1987, after only a month in Sittwe. When my mother appeared unannounced at her parents' home in Rangoon with my middle sister in her arms, her father had thought she had come back for good. *I knew you wouldn't be able to live there*, my grandfather said, *I told you not to go in the first place.* As a prank, my mother played along. She waited until my grandfather was done gloating to announce that she was in Rangoon only to interview for a scholarship.

The previous year, my mother had planned to go to England for graduate school. She had been accepted into a master's program for teaching English as a foreign language at the University of Warwick and had received a full scholarship from the Burmese government. When she became pregnant with my middle sister, however, she was forced to give up her scholarship and her spot in the program. My mother was devastated. During her pregnancy, she became obsessively focused on a single goal: to win another scholarship, to recover what she had lost, what she felt had been taken away from her. My mother's mother had dropped out of college to get married, and only returned to finish her degree years later after the birth of her fourth child. I think my mother wanted a different life from my grandmother's. I think she wanted to prove that she did not have to choose between a family and a career. She could have my sister and a master's degree. She could be a mother and still have dreams that were hers alone.

My mother's dream, when she lived in Sittwe, was to go abroad. In Bamar, the word meant another country, an other country. My mother said many Rakhine thought of my family as having come from abroad. They thought of Rangoon as a foreign capital and Burma as a foreign state. My mother often referred to Sittwe as *a place not even considered Burma*. She believed she had been transferred to such a place because it was her kan to go abroad. My parents were both fervent believers in kan, which they translated as luck, but which I came to understand as karma or fate. My mother believed she had the kan to go abroad, but because she had given up her scholarship, because she had not gone to England, she had been sent to Sittwe instead. The place most foreign to her within national borders.

Every day, my mother road a sidecar along the Kispanadi River to teach at Sittwe Degree College. A sidecar was the clever Bamar word for a kind of rickshaw with a passenger seat attached to one side of the bicycle. This daily commute by sidecar was the only image I had of my mother in Sittwe. The bicycle pedaled expertly by its owner, racing the river itself, and my mother, being used to city buses, not yet immune to the excitement of it all: the cool, humid air rushing at her face, the dark waters of the Kispanadi a viscous, opaque mass, and the sky equally obscure, a block of gray threatening rain.

The sidecar ride along the river was also, I think, the only image my mother had of Sittwe. With all the flying back and forth to Rangoon and the stormy weather and the protests and the school closures, my mother did not get to see much of the city or the rest of Rakhine State. She had wanted to see the white sand and clear turquoise waters of Ngapali Beach. She had wanted to visit the Mahamuni Buddha Temple in Kyauktaw. According to Buddhist legend, the Mahamuni Buddha image was made when the Buddha himself visited the ancient kingdom of Arakan, the region that was now present-day Rakhine State. The Mahamuni Buddha image was said to be one of the only likenesses of the Buddha made during his lifetime. When the Bamar conquered Arakan centuries ago, the original statue was taken to Mandalay, which was then the capital of the Burmese kingdom. The Rakhine king replaced the lost statue with a replica and a new legend grew around the new Mahamuni Buddha image. Whoever visited the temple in Kyauktaw three times and prayed three times for what they wanted would have their wish granted.

My mother wanted to visit the Mahamuni Buddha Temple in Kyauktaw so she could have her wish to go abroad be granted. Kyauktaw was north along the Kispanadi River, which farther upstream was called the Kaladan River. On a map, the town seemed relatively close to Sittwe, but without a car, or a boat, and with two small children to care for, my mother could not manage the trip. *All I saw of Rakhine State was our apartment*, my mother said.

In their apartment, she put up a photograph of the Kyauktaw Mahamuni Buddha image on her altar and prayed to it, very intently, three times on three different occasions. My mother hoped that the image's power of wish fulfillment would still work despite the many layers of representation. A photograph of a replica of a likeness. My mother had faith in the power of translation, of rebirth, in the idea that despite whatever was lost across languages, bodies, and lives, there remained something essential, something untouched and untouchable, that could still be transmitted.

The one place my mother did visit in Sittwe was Point, which was what the locals called Sittwe View Point, the southernmost tip of the city where the river emptied into the ocean. There was a beach there, my mother said, *at the mouth of the sea*, except in Bamar the phrase was more beautiful, *the opening of the sea*, or *the threshold of the sea*.

For my eldest sister's third birthday, in February of 1987, the family went down to the beach at Point to celebrate. My mother even brought two separate outfits in which to photograph the birthday girl. In one portrait, my sister is wearing a pleated red dress and white flip-flops, and in the other, she is in a bouncy white dress and turquoise sandals with bunnies on them. In both photographs, my sister is bedecked in a hat made of flowers, and seashell necklaces and bracelets too big for her little wrists. She looks like a happy toddler at the beach.

The photographs were misleading, however, because my eldest sister was not happy in Sittwe. My mother said my father had to take my sister on outings to Point regularly to cheer her up. Back in their apartment, my mother said my sister spent whole days lying on the large pine chest they had brought from Rangoon, barely moving at all. My eldest sister herself claimed to remember this. *I lay on that chest*, my sister said, *because I didn't want to touch anything else in that apartment.* The pine chest and the other luggage my parents had brought from Rangoon were all my sister had left of home.

It was my mother's wish, her dream, to go abroad, but she had no intention of leaving the country forever. This was a fact both of my parents took pride in: *we never wanted to abandon our country.* They had gone to Sittwe because they believed it was their patriotic duty. They believed the Rakhine were their countrymen and -women and worked to earn their respect. *The Rakhine were fond of us,* my parents always said proudly, *even though they hated most Bamar.* My parents believed they could make a difference. They believed in duty and courage and sacrifice, in the post-independence dream of a peaceful and prosperous multiethnic Burma.

Even back then, in the late eighties, my parents must have known, or at least feared, that this dream would never come to fruition. They must have known that the Burmese Way to Socialism was leading the country to ruin, that it was a catastrophic failure, and anyone with the means to leave the country was getting out. My father's elder sister had married an American tourist she met while working at the US embassy and had left the country years ago. My father's younger sister went to England on a government scholarship to get her bachelor's and never returned. In March of 1987, while my parents were in Sittwe, my father's mother and father also left to be with my aunt in America. *I did the math,* my mother said, *and your grandmother would have been sixty-three when she came here. The same age I am now.*

Though my mother never made it to the Mahamuni Buddha Temple in Kyauktaw, on her thirtieth birthday, in November of 1987, her neighbor, an older woman who took my mother under her wing, brought her to a large monastery in Sittwe. In my family, when I was growing up, birthdays were celebrated not with parties but with visits to the monastery where acts of good merit would be performed: donations of money and food for the monks, or, if one was lucky and there was a retreat taking place, for all the meditators as well. I was taught that a birthday was a time to give back, not to ask for presents or wishes.

My mother, however, went to the monastery in Sittwe to make a wish, which is what prayer translates to in Bamar, su taung, to ask for a prize or a reward. My mother's wish, of course, was to have another opportunity to go abroad, another scholarship, or anything else, any chance to leave Sittwe. The monk my mother's friend introduced her to did not understand why my mother wanted to leave. *Why can't you stay?* he asked her, and she did not know how to answer without giving offense. *I am just used to living in Rangoon,* she finally said. I wonder if my mother felt any guilt or shame in that moment, knowing that a life that was livable for the monk and everyone else was not livable for her. I think it is more likely, however, that I am projecting my own guilt and my own shame onto my mother. She never had enough privilege to feel ashamed, only grateful.

In the one photograph there is of my family in Sittwe, they are at Point, on a rare sunny day. The sea is calm and blue behind them. My mother and father are each holding a child. My father is wearing a paso, and a white collarless shirt, with the top buttons unbuttoned. He gives a closed-lip smile and holds my infant middle sister tightly in his arms. My sister stares straight at the camera with a mixture of curiosity and distrust, her chubby little body turned away from my father so she can get a better look. The pink sock on her left foot seems to be coming loose. My mother is radiant in a matching htamein and blouse set in a rich shade of blue. The kind of blue that is deserving of a more beautiful name, azure, or lapis lazuli. She holds up the htamein, or skirt, with one hand, so as not to get it wet, and with the other hand, she holds my eldest sister, who is in her white birthday outfit. My mother smiles for the camera, but my sister seems to be caught in a moment of panic. She is gripping a plastic yellow lunchbox tight in one hand and is pressing her other elbow against my mother's chest. My sister's pretty little mouth is opened wide, and her brown legs are swinging in the air. She seems to be afraid of touching the wet sand, or any part of Sittwe. She looks like she is about to cry.

Hinthada

In the only photograph ever taken of my great-grandfather and great-grandmother, they are seated in teak chairs, my great-grandfather with his elbows on the armrests, his hands lightly grazing his knees. His hands fine and plump, the left hand adorned with a large ring, the fingertips bearing its weight, and the right hand hanging heavy from the wrist.

My great-grandmother holds a flower in her right hand and her left rests on the seat of her chair, as if she is preparing to stand, or else has just steadied herself. Her necklace is askew, caught in the button of her blouse, and she looks at the camera with pained forbearance, as if the photograph were taken in the last moment before she exhaled a long-held breath.

This photograph hangs over the bookshelf in the room I used to share with my two sisters. For many years, I looked at it as if looking into a mirror, as if by my looking I could conjure the ghosts of my great-grandfather and my great-grandmother. I looked and looked at this photograph until I felt as if we were the ghosts, my middle sister and I, we, the remnants of these people.

I do not know if my great-grandfather was buried in Leymyethna, or cremated, or if his ashes were brought back to Hinthada and kept inside his trunk along with the family jewels. I do not know how much ash is produced when a body is burned. Ash is the remainder, the residue, the remnant or trace, the vestige of a body after it has burned. Ash is what could not burn, or what had to be created so something else could be destroyed. In this way, we are all each other's ashes. I am my great-grandfather's ash. I am the story that was told about his death, or the story that was created from his death, though many years later. I do not know the stories that were told at the time of his death. What my great-grandmother told her seven children, what she told herself.

My mother said my great-grandmother and great-grandfather had loved each other. They had had a happy marriage. She said when two people loved each other as much as my great-grandparents did, they usually died within days or weeks of each other and were reborn in the same womb, as twins. My great-grandfather, however, died too young, and too unexpectedly. He was only a little over forty. My great-grandmother could not follow him into death, not yet; she still had seven children to raise. My great-grandmother was a few years older than my great-grandfather, my mother said, two or three years, the same as the age gap between my middle sister and me. My great-grandfather would have had to call his wife ma, meaning big sister, and she would have had to call him maung, little brother. In Bamar, all polite pronouns are familial; to speak the language is to become a part of a family. I call my eldest sister ma, but not my middle sister. Though she is three years older than me, she was so small, and I grew so quickly, that for most of our childhood and adolescence, we were always mistaken for twins.

When my great-grandmother and her children returned home to Hinthada, they discovered that the house they had left behind was exactly the same. Untouched by the British bombs and the Japanese bombs, untouched by looters, soldiers, and wild animals. It was as if the war had never happened, as if the family had never left. The house was pristine, immaculate, pyu cin, like my eldest sister's name, meaning white and clean. A new beginning.

It was a miracle, my mother said, a testament to my great-grandmother's faith, the power of her faith, her prayers of protection. I think it would have been a greater miracle if my great-grandfather had not died. If my great-grandmother's prayers could have protected him instead of the house. But I know prayers do not work in that way. I know that all beings are owners of their actions. My great-grandfather died because he had to, because all of us have to die someday. Many of their neighbors' homes were destroyed, my mother said my great-grandmother said. Some of their neighbors never returned.

As a widow, my great-grandmother was protective of her children. Every night, she walked through the house casting prayers so the family jewels would not be robbed, and her daughters would not be violated. The jewels were kept locked in the attic, and the daughters were kept hidden inside the house. For seven years they were not allowed to leave the house. They were not allowed to go to school.

For years Ohnmardani was kept hidden inside her parents' house, because of her beauty. Patacara too was locked away for the same reason. Subha, because she was not locked away, was harassed by a libertine, a philanderer, a rake. There are many euphemisms in English for men who perpetrate sexual violence, and only one word for rapist. I do not even know that word in Bamar. The only words I know are everyday ones, common ones. He insulted her. He wronged her. To escape from her harasser, her potential rapist, Subha plucked out her eye and gave it to him. Because she was enlightened, she felt no pain, and later the eye was restored. All three stories end in the same way: the women achieve enlightenment. They become fearless.

My great-grandmother was fearful. She sent her sons to school and kept her daughters at home because that was what was done, that was what the British did. Gentlemen's daughters were educated at home. My grandmother and her sisters, though, were a gentleman's orphans, and there was no money for a governess or a tutor. There was no money, but there was the large house they lived in, and the family jewels, the royal jewels that my great-grandfather had inherited from his mother. My great-grandmother sold the jewels, one by one. She loaned out the money she made from these sales and collected interest. She took in boarders at the house. My grandmother, the eldest daughter, was in charge of all the bookkeeping. She was good with numbers. My grandmother was a very capable, very efficient and organized person. That was what my mother always said, and what I observed the two times I met her as a child. Her clothes were always crisp and clean, her hair perfectly in place, and the jasmines pinned in it always fresh.

When my great-grandmother finally died, she was reborn as my middle sister. My sister was my wife in our past life. My mother says I followed her into this life. My mother believes my sister was once my great-grandmother because of the dream she had before my sister's birth and also because after my sister was born, she displayed the same traits and mannerisms that my great-grandmother once possessed. A peculiar way of wiping one's mouth, with the thumb and forefinger rather than the back of the hand. Miserliness. Irritability. Stubbornness. As a toddler my sister carried on fights with my grandmother that had started in a past life when my grandmother was her daughter. My sister furrowed her brows, hunched her back, and frowned. My mother always called my sister *a little old lady*. My sister even looked like my great-grandmother. She had the same small and slender frame, the same fair skin, the same unmistakable beauty.

My middle sister traveled to Hinthada to see her old house and re-turned with artifacts from our previous life: a striped skinny tie that once belonged to our great-grandfather, our great-grandmother's music box. The house had been damaged by the cyclone, but our great-aunt who still lived in Hinthada was making repairs. The house that had withstood Japanese and British bombs had not with-stood Nargis. The roof had flown off, and the contents of the attic were lost, including my eldest sister's beloved stuffed bear.

My middle sister also brought back the photograph that now hangs above the bookshelf in our old room, the room I used to share with my sisters. I do not know how old they were when the picture was taken, how many children they had already had, how close they were to war, to death. After all these years, I still cannot make out what is in the background of the photograph: a threshold to an-other room, frames leaned against the wall, or a dark mirror that shows no reflection.

Ghosts live inside of mirrors, my mother always said, and when we were young, she warned that looking into a mirror was even worse for your eyes than watching television. There was once a young, beautiful woman, my mother said, but she was very vain, and she spent all her time looking into a mirror and admiring her beauty, until she ruined her eyes and finally went blind. I do not remember if the woman then perished, or if she repented and shaved her head.

Our family monk asked me if I wanted him to read my fortune and I knew it was a trick question because monks did not tell fortunes. Holy men believed in karma, not superstition. My mother always said so before she gave a reading of any kind, and my father always said so when he wanted to wash his hair on a Wednesday. I did not know how to answer the monk. I could feel my whole family watching me, waiting for me to speak. Finally, the monk said, *here is your fortune. You will grow old. You will get sick and you will die.* I knew, even then, that the monk was wrong. Many people do not grow old or get sick. They just die.

A few years ago, I made a list of everyone I knew who had died, in chronological order. My uncle who died of liver failure. My grandmother who died of diabetes. My grandfather who died of pneumonia. My friend in high school who died in a car accident when the driver fell asleep at the wheel. Another uncle who also died of liver failure. A boy in my freshman-year dorm who fell off the roof of a building and died. A girl in my anthropology class who was reported dead, though I never found out how she died. My aunt who had a heart attack. A friend of a friend who walked into the bay and drowned himself. My grandfather and grandmother who died of old age. An old acquaintance whose death I only learned of years after we lost touch. Our family monk who died of lung cancer. A boy I knew from college who once told me he sometimes looks around a crowded room and wonders, *Who will love me?* He was found dead on the subway tracks at four in the morning.

And before all these deaths, my brother died. His death the first death in my life, though it occurred before my life began.

The first time my eldest sister pushed a finger down her throat, she said she thought of our brother, and how he had died because he vomited up all of his milk, because he could not drink, take nourishment, and grow. All the days he was in the hospital, my mother prayed that he would live. She was not allowed to see him at the hospital. My father and my grandparents would not allow it. They believed that women who had recently given birth were in a delicate state, a precarious state, of soft blood and soft skin, and in this state, they were close to madness. My father and my grandparents believed my mother had to be shielded from any shock or disturbance.

And my brother's body had been shocking, my mother said, when she finally saw him at the children's hospital, in an incubator at the intensive care unit. She hardly recognized him. He had been a fair, chubby baby, a handsome boy, and now he looked like a shriveled animal, so many tubes and wires sticking out of his little body. He would have fit in the palm of her hand, my mother said, her small, slender hand. But she was not allowed to hold him.

Vomiting was the activity of ghosts, my mother always said. Ghosts could not speak or touch or bleed, but they could vomit. Vomit and ghosts, the ultimate others, the abject, that which is rejected from the body, in death or in times of distress when reality is rejected: the image in the mirror, the weight of one's flesh on one's body of bones.

I never found the jars of vomit hidden in the closet I shared with my two sisters, but I always knew the closet was haunted. I always made sure the closet door was closed before I went to bed. My eldest sister vomited in jars because there was only one bathroom between the five of us and it wasn't easy for her to hide her illness. Though sometimes she didn't bother to hide it at all, and sometimes she used it as a weapon against my mother. She would lock herself in the bathroom in the middle of a fight, and neglect to turn on the fan, so that we could all hear what she was doing in there, so my mother could hear her son dying a second death, so she would be sorry for whatever she had said.

I remember watching my sister on her knees in the kitchen one evening. The cabinet below the sink swung open, the trash pulled out, and my sister's head bent over it. My mother said ghosts eat out of dumpsters and I believed my sister was possessed. I don't remember what excuse she gave me, but I remember I didn't believe it. I was old enough to recognize a lie. I said, *I've puked only once in my life.* Keep watching me, my sister said, and you'll be able to vomit too.

The first time my eldest sister pushed a finger down her throat, she thought of my brother and how he had died, how she had died, because that was the worst thing that had happened to her, that had happened to all of us daughters, long before we were born, and when she made herself vomit, it was as if she were bringing him back to life, by reliving his death, as if she were aborting him over and over again, so that in the moment before she bent her head over the toilet, or the trash in the kitchen, or the glass jar in her hands, in the dark of the closet, he was alive again, at the back of her throat, a ghost waiting to be born.

That night at the hospital, my mother changed her prayers. She no longer prayed for my brother's life, she said, but for an end to his suffering.

Until very recently, I had vomited only once in my life. I remember little of the incident, only having gone to bed nauseated, then waking up in the middle of the night, and suddenly my parents there in the bathroom with me, my father holding me up by the sink, and the feeling of disgust and relief when I dribbled out a yellowish paste. It felt like crying, but even better and worse, and still half-asleep it was all a dream or a nightmare: my father's hands gripping my armpits, the fluorescent light above the mirror, and the shadows everywhere else.

Gayan

Shortly after my grandfather's father died from the loss of land, his eldest brother, a boy of sixteen or seventeen who had been acting as the man of the family, died as well and my grandfather was sent to live with his uncle in Rangoon.

Rangoon was a port city newly established as the capital at the end of three wars fought over nearly a century. My great-grandfather's uncle worked for the victors, the British, as most people did in the city. He was an inspector of distilleries. My grandfather was sent to a private Bamar-language school along with his cousins. The government schools taught only English. At the government schools, students had to pray, wear Western clothes, and take English names. Children were stripped of their unique names and called by an English first name followed by their father's name.

My mother's father had gone to a colonial government school. His unique name was Win Kyaing and his father's was Ba Cho. At school, my mother's father became Walter Ba Cho. The boy Win Kyaing was erased. But my father's father was not erased. At the Bamar-language school, he was allowed to keep his unique name, Kyaw Myint. I do not even remember the name of his father. It is a relief, to be able to forget the names of the fathers.

My grandfather wanted an education because he wanted to own something that could not be lost, to a gambling brother-in-law, to debt collectors, to fires, floods, kings, thieves, and the other calamities of existence. At the Bamar-language school, my father said, the children were taught not only Bamar, English, math, science, and history, but also patriotism, which in Bamar translated not to love for country but love for a people. Love for myo, my father's name and my own, meaning relative, kin, race, nation, and people. I do not know who is a part of this people and who is apart from them. I do not think I will ever learn.

A few years before my grandfather would graduate from high school, his uncle, his guardian in Rangoon, died, unexpectedly on one of his inspection rounds. A drunk man stabbed and killed him. My grandfather's aunt was plunged into suffering, my father said. She entered the story only after her husband's death, as if she were his ghost. My grandfather's aunt suffers her husband's untimely death and my grandfather suffers as well. His education comes to an end before it is complete, and he is sent back home.

When my grandfather returned to Gayan, the countryside was ravaged. The term my father used, pyet see, meant ruined, damaged, or destroyed. Pyet, to break or to lose. My grandfather's family were no longer landowners and no longer wealthy. My grandfather's brothers were their father's sons and did not know how to farm the land that was left to them, how to work the land, how to live off it. My great-grandmother did not know either.

My grandfather's uncle was the third man in his life to die an untimely death, the third father figure. I wonder if my grandfather returned to Gayan, where my grandfather's father and elder brother had died, so he could die as well. I wonder if my grandfather thought that was what men did, what it meant to be a man. I wonder if he joined the army, the resistance, because he hoped it would kill him.

My grandfather returned to Gayan without his high school diploma, but because he had any education at all, soon after he joined the Burmese Independence Army, he was promoted to the rank of lieutenant. In Gayan, my father said, there were *no schools, nothing, not even today*. I could not find the village on any map, and do not even know if it still exists. My grandfather and two other officers, the only educated men in Gayan, were given a hundred men to command. My grandfather was only sixteen years old.

Meanwhile, back in Rangoon, Bogyoke Aung San, the former student activist and revolutionary turned general, addressed the Burmese army. It was not the Burmese Independence Army, which my grandfather had joined, but the army that the Japanese had created in its place a year later, the Burma Defense Army, which was then later renamed the Burma National Army.

Names change often when a country is created by men. Men know that names, that words, hold power. This is why they impose their names on women. They know that an independence army can exist only before independence has been won, that a national army implies there is already a nation. In 1945, the Japanese wanted to signal that independence had already been won, that Asia had been returned to Asians, and that a new nation had already been established. Despite what the Japanese called the army, none of this was true. Burmese people had simply exchanged one foreign colonizer for another.

In his speech to the army, Bogyoke Aung San commanded his men to *kill the nearest enemy*. My father repeated those words as if he heard them himself, though they were spoken more than a decade before his birth. The nearest enemy meant the Japanese. The soldiers understood what their general meant. They fled to the mountains. The Japanese forces were better trained, better armed, and better provisioned than the Burmese army, which was mostly composed of young volunteers like my grandfather. The only advantages the Burmese had were the land and the climate. The densely forested Bago Yoma and the rain that seemed not to fall from the sky, but to spring up from the ground itself.

The land did most of the killing for them, my father said my grandfather said. The Japanese soldiers my grandfather fought were already mostly dead. Starving because they could find no food, in the abandoned villages they passed or in the mountains. The villages were abandoned because the villagers fled and hid when they learned the Japanese were approaching. The villagers took their stores of food and destroyed what they had to leave behind. The men my grandfather killed had not eaten for weeks. They could barely walk, my father said, much less fight. Some of them did not even have the strength to carry their guns. I imagined they dragged their guns behind them, through the mud of the jungle, or leaned on them like canes. I imagine the Japanese soldiers were young men, though aged by hunger and disease. *It was nothing to be proud of killing men like that*, my grandfather told my father. Men who were already dead. The only dead man I have seen is my grandfather, lying in a casket, as if asleep.

My father's favorite story to tell was the one about how my grandfather's life was saved by a chicken. One day, a nearby village sent over a chicken for my grandfather and the other two officers to eat. A live chicken. A rare meal in those days of hiding in the jungle. The Burmese soldiers were not starving the way the Japanese were, but they were not eating well either.

My grandfather did not trust his men to cook the chicken for him. He did not trust that they would not eat most of it while they cooked. My grandfather was a glutton, my father said, so he took on the task of cooking the chicken himself. As he was tending to his pot of chicken, a villager brought news of ten Japanese soldiers nearby. My grandfather and the other officers had a hundred men between them. A hundred men against ten Japanese soldiers. They knew that their men wanted to fight, that they were tired of only killing men who were nearly dead. The other two officers decided to fight, but my grandfather's chicken was not yet ready, so he stayed behind. All one hundred of the men left.

In a little while, before the chicken was even ready, they stumbled back to camp, the survivors. There was only a third of them left, maybe thirty men. They said to my grandfather, *Lieutenant, we have to run.* The ten Japanese soldiers that the villager had reported were only the scouts. There were three hundred more men behind them. Three hundred well-armed and well-trained Japanese soldiers. The Burmese men had no training, the officers themselves had none. They were all slaughtered. The other two officers died, shot and killed. Most of the men under my grandfather's command died as well. Those who were left, his men and the men of the two officers who had died, fled deeper into the jungle, higher up the mountains. But my grandfather did not leave the chicken behind. He had two of his soldiers lug the pot between them.

I wonder how my grandfather's chicken tasted. I wonder where he learned to cook. If his mother ever taught him, or his aunt in Rangoon. I wonder if this chicken from the village was the first meal he had ever cooked for himself. I doubt he had spices hiding in the jungle, that he had fish sauce, so far from the ocean, from the delta where he was born. I wonder if he missed Rangoon, or if he missed Gayan. I wonder if being so far from home, it was as if his father and his brother were still alive, as if they had never died, as if they would be waiting for him when he returned, along with his mother and younger brothers. I wonder if he could forget that the land had ever been sold, the family land he was meant to inherit. I wonder if he could forget that anything bad had ever happened to him before the war. If the chicken tasted like chicken he had eaten as a boy, chicken that the family cook had prepared, if she had been the one who taught him how to cook.

But it is more likely that the chicken tasted like death, an animal he had killed with his own hands, hands that had killed men. The chicken was meant to be shared between him and the other two officers. The two men who died while the chicken was cooking.

I also wonder about the bodies of the dead. The men that my grandfather killed, or his men who were killed in turn. I wonder if they were burned or buried, or if they were left to rot. In the jungle, I imagine the dead decompose quickly. In the jungle there are tigers and leopards and pythons, bacteria and microorganisms that emerge from the ground and consume the dead with invisible mouths. I imagine it is a dangerous place to lie down. But I don't want to imagine the jungle only as a place glutted with death. To my grandfather and his men it was also their home. The jungle, the forest, the wilderness, the taw. My father called Gayan a taw myot, a town in the wilderness, in the forest, in the jungle. Gayan, a jungle town, where my grandfather was born, a small village. My mother used to call my father a taw tha to tease him. Taw tha, son of the taw, a peasant. It was mostly these men who died in the war, sons of the jungle. Their bodies fed the living land.

And the land tried to claim my grandfather's body as well. At the end of the war, just as he was about to descend from the mountains, to leave the jungle, he was seized by a malarial fever, the kind that had killed many men during the war. For a full month, my grandfather was too sick to travel, sick with the bird fever, as the disease is called in Bamar.

I did not know why malaria was called bird disease when the sickness was spread by mosquitoes, not birds. My mother said it is not because birds spread the disease, but because birds can be infected by it as well. Avian malaria. I never liked birds. I did not like their clawed feet, or their sharp beaks, or their black, vacant eyes. Their corpses littering the street, flattened, like inkblots on paper, blood smeared on the asphalt. Once, as a child, I accidentally stepped on and killed a baby bird and I have since been afraid of birds, dead ones, falling from the sky. It is a nightmare I often have. The heaviness of their bodies, dropping to the earth. When I see birds in the sky, I can think only of that, the weight of their bodies, suspended in the air.

My grandfather dropped like a dead bird, but then he rose again. His fever broke. He recovered, survived, and lived, to return from the mountains, and the war.

Madrid

In Madrid two things were in abundance: metro stops and convenience stores. The convenience stores sold everything: snacks, toiletries, school supplies, even socks and underwear. This is why they are called convenience stores in North America. In Spain, they were called chinos. They were run almost exclusively by East Asian families. She did not know if the families were even Chinese. She did not know if they owned the stores. She could only guess at how they felt about the term chino.

Sometimes she entered the stores for the pure pleasure of listening to other Asian people speak Spanish. When a teenage son or daughter was at the register, she was especially pleased. Then, she was afflicted with guilt. She remembered all the well-meaning people in her life who had remarked on how well she spoke English. The enthusiasm in their voice. The biases they betrayed. She remembered how much she resented them and how much she resented this language, which was her native tongue, though not the only one.

And to have two native tongues is to have a split tongue, a forked tongue, to be duplicitous, as in deceitful, dishonest, disingenuous, though the prefix dipl- only means twofold, double, two-faced, Janus-faced, double-dealing. It is unacceptable to be two things at once, to see both sides, to not choose one or the other. To be both a man and a woman, a native and a foreigner, the oppressed and the oppressor.

She cannot remember why she chose to apply for a fellowship to Spain when she could have gone anywhere in the world. In her application, she had written about García Lorca's *Poet in New York* as if that book meant something to her, when it did not. She had been to New York only a handful of times when she was in college and had despised the city. Maybe that had been her connection to Lorca. Or maybe going to Spain was for her a way of returning to the motherland, the heart of the empire, the country of namesakes. She had spent her childhood going on field trips to nearby missions and even built a model of Mission San Juan Bautista in the fourth grade, out of Styrofoam and cardboard. During the project, she remembers her mother said, *If I had grown up in this country, I would have failed every class.*

When she arrived in Madrid, at the airport on the outskirts of the city, the landscape did remind her of where she grew up. The bald, dry earth and the dark green shrubs clinging to it, the low trees, foothills in the distance. Only, instead of strip malls and ranch-style homes, there was Madrid, the capital city, with its promenades and plazas and roundabouts, which were handsomely named glorietas. The city's grandeur made her feel small but important, as if she were the protagonist of a Hemingway novel with some gorgeous, lyrical title. She had never felt more American in her life.

She soon learned, however, that many people in the city thought she was Chinese. She walked down the street and people shouted *china, china* to get her attention. Street vendors, people advertising nightclubs, people trying to lure customers into their restaurants. Once, a teacher at the school where she worked asked if she would tutor the teacher's child in Chinese. Her roommate's son said she should have taken the job. *You could have made something up*, he said. She was annoyed at being mistaken for Chinese because she did not think she looked Chinese at all. If people were going to shout at her on the street, she thought, they should at least make a better guess. Whenever she was mistaken for Filipina, or Cambodian, or Laotian, or Latina, or Native American, it was usually by people who identified as such, and she felt almost complimented. No Chinese person had ever thought she was Chinese. This was probably because China and Burma shared a border.

She did not expect anyone to take her for an American. She did not even wish it. She was embarrassed by the American tourists on the metro, their fanny packs and sunburns, how they seemed to assume that no one around them could understand English, loudly appraising the city the same way she had once heard boys at a fraternity evaluating female party guests. She did not feel much camaraderie with her compatriots on the fellowship, either. Many had come straight from college and acted as if they were on an extended spring break, or, worse, an anthropological field study. They complained about the slow service at restaurants and long lines at the bank as if these were moral failings on the part of Spaniards. Her roommate's son, her first friend in the city, used to laugh at the word Spaniard, how unsexy it sounded compared to español, which she agreed was smooth and sinuous. With her roommate's son, and her one other Spanish friend, she derided all of America's faults as she perceived them: monolingualism, consumerism, imperialism, political apathy. Behind her rants was real shame. She felt it when her roommate's son revealed that his college tuition amounted to a little over a thousand euros a year, when a teacher at the school where she worked took a full sixteen weeks of paid maternity leave, when she went to the doctor for an upper-respiratory infection and there was no co-payment for her visit or medication. The dream among her American friends, the few she made, was to find a Spanish boyfriend and a reason to stay. But really, she did not want to stay, despite all the benefits. She did not want to become a bitter expat, to take up smoking and lose her accent, even though she suspected that this was the only way she could ever become fully American. Only in a foreign country could she feel that she belonged to hers.

Halfway through her year in Madrid, a friend from college who was Chinese American visited her for a few days. She does not remember anyone yelling *china, china* to her friend in the streets, but she does remember her friend telling her stories about men mistaking her friend as part white. One story was about a man on a bus and another story was about a man in a lecture hall. She was baffled by why her friend was sharing these stories, as if they were interesting or funny, with almost a touch of pride. For a brief moment, she felt as if she had missed something, a joke or a twist, and then she remembered. She had heard similar stories before, from a girl in high school who had gone to Hong Kong one summer. That girl had recounted, in the same tone, with the same carefully contained excitement, how many people in Hong Kong had asked her if her father was white. That was the detail she remembered, that people had asked specifically about the girl's father.

Earlier or later, she offered to let her friend borrow her ID card so her friend could visit museums for free while she went to work. The friend laughed at the suggestion. *I can't pretend to be you*, the friend said. She tried to argue. It was true, they did not actually look alike, but they were both Asian and they were in Spain, so it would not matter. *But you are so much darker than me*, the friend said, and held out her pale arm for comparison.

Or maybe her friend had not held out an arm, and she had only imagined it because the gesture was so familiar to her. Maybe her friend had said instead, *if I were three shades darker*, or *but I am so much lighter*. Her memory is inexact. She cannot remember, for example, how she responded, how the remainder of the visit went, how she and this friend eventually stopped being friends.

When she was a child, there were women, often nearly strangers, always white, who expressed envy for her skin color, which they described as *tanned*. These women would grab and stroke her arm, lament about how many hours in the sun or the tanning bed they would have to spend to achieve her hue. This rarely happened when she actually did have a tan, when her skin turned deep and rich. Only her mother dared to comment on her skin then, teasingly calling her a dark-skinned ruby stone. When she asked what that meant, her mother said that though light skin was the standard of beauty, dark skin was considered precious, a mark of value. The last queen of Burma and her daughters had all been dark.

Toward the end of her time in Madrid, people stopped asking her if she was Chinese and began asking if she was Ecuadorian or Peruvian or Nicaraguan. This made her happy. She thought it meant her Spanish had improved. At the time, she did not consider why speaking poor Spanish was equated with being Asian. She did not consider how speaking poor English was also equated with being Asian. How being a foreigner anywhere, an other, was often equated with being Asian. Asia, the East, the Orient, the exotic land behind a mirror where everything is backward and upside down. At the time, she did not consider all this. She was just pleased to hear elderly ladies call her bonita and guapa, to hear them tell her, *Wherever you're from, you're beautiful.*

She was born in the Chinese year of the snake. She does not know what snakes symbolize according to the Chinese zodiac, but in the Buddhist stories she knows, snakes are related to nagas, giant shapeshifting serpents, half-human and half-ophidian, with magical powers. Her parents translated naga into English as dragon. It made sense to her. The year of the dragon precedes the year of the snake. She thought snakes were simply dragons who had lost their wings. She thought they had forked tongues because they were shape-shifters, part dragon, part human, part mortal, and part divine. In school, it was not the story of Eve and the serpent that captured her imagination, but the story of la serpiente emplumada, Quetzalcoatl, a deity for whom Cortés believed he was mistaken. She always hated that myth, which made Moctezuma out to be gullible and superstitious, deserving of his tragic fate, as Eve deserved her banishment from Eden. She could not conceive what it must have been like for the conquistadors, to believe that wherever you went, you were a god.

Sittwe

For a long time, I believed I was conceived in Sittwe, in the haunted government apartment where the electricity only came on at night and the water only ran in the early morning. I believed I was conceived under the city's perpetually gray skies, perhaps on a rainy day, perhaps even in the midst of a tropical storm. My parents always spoke of Sittwe as a place of exile, a place of banishment, and as someone who had lived all the life I could remember in places where I was an exile, an immigrant against my will, it gave me comfort to believe that my life had begun in Sittwe, far from home. Somehow, it was easier to believe that I was conceived in a foreign place than in Rangoon, where I was born, and where my mother was born before me.

I have no memories of Rangoon. I cannot remember my mother's parents' house where my family first lived, or the small house they later built and moved into, on my father's parents' land. Growing up, I heard so many stories of these places that it almost felt like they were a part of me too. I knew that my mother's parents' house was actually on the Pyi Thar Yar side of the railroad, but when my mother was young, Pyi Thar Yar was not as well-known of a neighborhood as Bauk Htaw, so she grew up saying she was from Bauk Htaw. I knew that when my grandparents first bought the house, nothing west of the railroad was developed, it was just a quiet, open area, but now Yangon has expanded, and Pyi Thar Yar has become a bustling urban neighborhood. I knew that Saw Bwar Gyi Gone, where my father's parents lived, was in the northern part of the city, almost an hour away from my mother's parents' house by bus. I knew it was close to the international airport and to Rangoon Institute of Technology, but also close to Insein Township and Insein Prison, which even then was notorious as a place of torture.

I knew all this, but unlike my sisters, I had no memories of playing in my mother's parents' garden, chasing my grandfather from banana tree to banana tree. I had no memories of riding a tricycle through the wooded acres of my father's parents' backyard. I had only a few family photographs to prove that I was really there, that once there was a time when I had lived in a house my parents built, on land that my grandparents owned.

Though I was not conceived in Sittwe, it was in Sittwe that a bay-din saya, an astrologer, told my mother that she would get her wish to go abroad only after she had another child. My mother was distressed by this prediction. She had not been planning to have a third child. She had not planned to have a second child or a first, either. My brother, my middle sister, and I were all, more or less, happy accidents. Only my eldest sister had been wanted, after the loss of my brother.

My mother did want me later on, though, after she had a dream, around the time of my conception, of a child lifting her out from an abyss, a pit into which she had fallen. *A lucky child*, my mother said, *a child sent by bodaws*. Bodaw was a title of respect for weikzas, holy beings with magical powers who lived in the woods and the moun-tains. Weikzas, my mother said, achieved near-immortal lifespans through meditation and other practices and many of them were waiting for the next Buddha to be born. The monk my mother's neighbor took her to in Sittwe was known for his ability to com-municate with weikzas. My mother said one could tell the weikzas had visited if the incense sticks in the monastery curled in a coil when they burned. The monk told my mother that weikzas looked after her and our family. My mother believed that I was a gift from them.

When the Phone Maw ayekhin broke out in March of 1988, my mother returned to her parents' house in Bauk Htaw with the children. *Anytime anything happened*, my mother said, *you'd find me back in Rangoon.* The school year ended in February, so my mother had been in staying in Sittwe only to be with my father, who had year-long duties as the English department chair. After a few months, during which the riot police shot at, killed, beat, and arrested hundreds of student demonstrators, my father was finally able to return to Rangoon as well. *It was right before things got to be very bad*, my mother said, *in June or July. You know what happened in August.*

My mother went to the airport on three different occasions with my sisters to pick up my father, and each time his flight was canceled. The airport was in Mingaladon, across the city from my mother's parents' house, past the university campuses where the marches had started, and past Inya Lake, where student protestors had drowned after the police opened fire on them. My mother said my father's flights were canceled because of my sisters' bad luck, but July was also the beginning of the rainy season, when the monsoon brought torrential rains, and it was more likely the flights had been canceled due to bad weather. The fourth time my mother went to the airport to pick up my father, she left my sisters in the care of my grandparents, and went alone. This time, my father's flight was on time. The plane landed safely and the family was reunited.

Before my father returned to Rangoon, my mother had been staying at her parents' house in Bauk Htaw. This was where my parents lived after they got married. Growing up, I heard many stories about my father's misadventures living with his in-laws. Once, he dropped a bar of soap into the well and the whole family got diarrhea. Another time, he threw a pressure cooker into the backyard, where it exploded. My mother referred to the house as the place where my brother was born, though he was born in a hospital. She meant it was the place where they lived when he was born, the place where he had lived, however briefly.

After my brother's death, my mother believed the house was cursed, that it was unlucky, that, in some way, it had killed my brother. Before my eldest sister was born, she had my grandparents' detached garage converted into an apartment. A second story was added, and the garage itself was lined with bricks to keep it cool.

The house my parents moved to after my father returned to Rangoon, the house where I was conceived, was one they had built themselves on my father's parents' land in Saw Bwar Gyi Gone right before they received their transfer orders to Sittwe. In the one photograph I have seen of the house, it looks like it is being swallowed by the ground, its uneven brick walls barely visible behind a mound of dirt and rocks. Only its tin roof, not yet rusted, shone aboveground. My mother said my father's older brother, who also lived on the land, forced them to build on low ground, practically in a ditch, because he did not want their house interrupting his view. Their house was built so low that a neighbor's dog once jumped on their roof and wouldn't come down. *It was a very bad omen*, my mother said.

On August 8, 1988, soon after my family reunited and resettled in the Saw Bwar Gyi Gone house, the country erupted in a nationwide strike and mass demonstrations, which came to be known as the 8888 ayekhin, or uprising. The strike was the culmination of several months of protests and marches that had been ongoing since March, and of several years, whole decades of enduring the military government's abuses, mismanagement, violence, and corruption. My grandparents remembered the student protests of 1962, when General Ne Win first seized power, and my parents remembered the protests in 1974 when UN secretary-general U Thant died and the government denied him a state burial. The 8888 ayekhin was larger than both of these movements and anything that came before. The demonstrations spread all over the country, even to Sittwe, where I imagine my parents' students at Sittwe Degree College were marching in the streets too. I never asked my parents why they did not join the demonstrations, but I already knew the answer. They had small children to care for, and they did not want to die.

I have always believed in my mother's prophetic dream that I was a lucky child, a child blessed by weikzas, the worship of whom, I later learned, was forbidden by the government at the time. I have always believed that I had more luck, more good fortune, than anyone else in my family because I was conceived in the short month of hope between the general strike on August 8 and the bloody crackdown that followed on September 18. But my mother said August had not been a hopeful month, but one of uncertainty and fear. *You were conceived in pure chaos*, my mother said. My father said the government had fostered an atmosphere of anarchy in order to justify the coup they had planned. Thousands of inmates from Insein Prison and other prisons around the country were released under mysterious circumstances, and my father and the other men in Saw Bwar Gyi Gone, which bordered Insein Township, had to organize a neighborhood watch. My mother said there were nights when everyone in the neighborhood hid together in a ditch when there were rumors of a raid. And in fact, there were riots and looting, especially of government property, which many people, including my parents, believed was carried out by the military itself. *It was anarchy*, my father said, *that's what the military wanted, so they could take over again.*

Every student protest in the past had ended with government forces opening fire on unarmed protestors. In September of 1988, two months after General Ne Win had resigned, the military staged a second coup. They declared martial law, and in cities all over the country, the military fired into crowds of peaceful protestors. In a farewell speech Ne Win gave on the day of his resignation back in July, he ominously foreshadowed this violence. *When the army shoots, it shoots to kill.* Thousands died and thousands more were injured, were arrested, were tortured, were disappeared. I do not know how many.

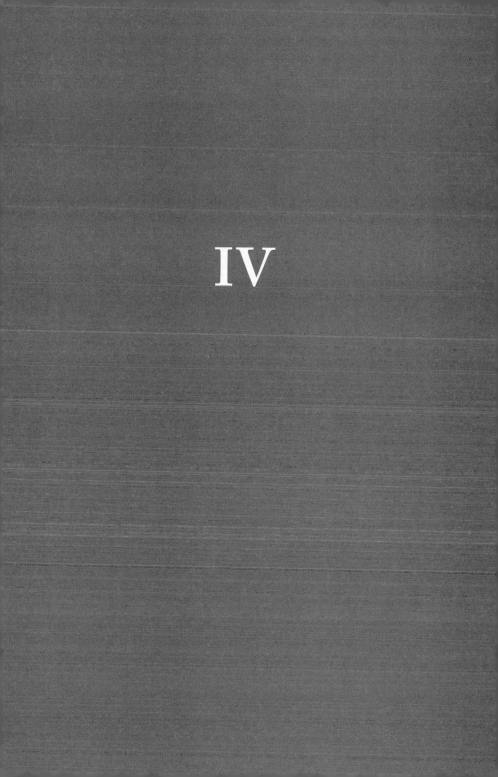

IV

Hinthada

I do not want to repeat the story I have heard, of how my grand-mother and her sisters were kept at home for seven years follow-ing the war. How they were not allowed to attend school. I am afraid it is the story you have been waiting for. I am afraid I have been given the opportunity to speak only because I am saying what you want to hear, what you wish you could say, what you are say-ing now, through my body, behind the protection my body offers with its brown skin, black eyes, and black hair. It is the story you have been telling for centuries now, of how brown women need to be saved from brown men, or even from brown parents, brown mothers. My great-grandmother was not brown-skinned like me. She was light-skinned, but she was not white, so it is all the same. Whiteness is not a color or a race or an ethnicity but a construct of power, the power to speak, to tell stories, not only about oneself, but about other people.

My grandmother had to protest to go back to school. She had to turn over the alms bowl, my mother said, to refuse what was freely given in exchange for what was withheld. My grandmother did not eat until her mother allowed her to return to school. Then, my grandmother walked to Hinthada High School by herself and enrolled in standard 9. She had only passed standard 7 before the war, but she skipped standard 8 and took the standard 9 and standard 10 exams in one year. *How old was she?* I asked my mother. *Around twenty*, my mother said. The age when a novice monastic can become fully ordained, the age when one comes of age.

Once, a white man said to me, you are so privileged you might as well be white. We were in Italy, this man and I, for a conference entirely paid for by the university we both attended. In line for pastries at breakfast, the man—who, at the time, I thought of as only a boy, a classmate, and a friend—confided in me that this was his first time in Europe. He then asked me where I had been in Europe, and when I told him—the Netherlands, Spain, France, Portugal, the Czech Republic, Lithuania—he delivered his pronouncement, with real disdain, though masked as a joke, because, after all, we were friends.

When my grandmother graduated from high school, she had to protest again in order to go on to university. Another hunger strike, another fight with her mother. She was twenty-four when she was finally allowed to go to Rangoon.

At the end of my grandmother's second year at the University of Rangoon, her aunt and uncle decided that it was time for her to be married, that she was educated enough for a woman. The man they had in mind for my grandmother worked under her uncle in the Income Tax Department. He was an income tax officer, nine years older than my grandmother. She saw him once at the Shwedagon Pagoda, and he saw her, and from a distance they each decided the other was suitable. They did not speak until their wedding day.

I do not want to tell this story about my grandmother because I am afraid it is the only story I am allowed to tell. Brown woman locked up, hidden away, uneducated, and married off. The moral of the story is: look how much better off we are. Look at me, the granddaughter, free to pursue her Western education, free to marry the white man she loves. The first time I met my mother-in-law she asked, *How are women treated in your culture?* I am the woman who has emerged from my great-grandmother's house to answer this question, to tell my grandmother's story. After seven years and two generations, after crossing oceans and nations, I have emerged so I can be put on display, proudly, as a token of civilization and progress. Look at how much better off I am.

My mother said her father used to boast that he respected her mother's uncle so much he would have married anyone the man suggested. My grandmother hated my grandfather. She used to tell my mother all the ways she would torture him once he got old and sick and had to depend on her. All the ways she would seek her revenge. She was sure that he would be the first to die, since he was nine years older. It was only on her deathbed that she forgave him, forgave him with her eyes when she could no longer speak. My mother was not present when my grandmother died, but my aunt told her that their father had been very sweet, very tender and devoted, that he had never left their mother's side. He had loved her, and my grandmother did not know it until the end.

Years later, a friend and I are trading stories over lunch, and I tell him about the time I was told I might as well be white. I tell my friend that I feel ashamed of how I responded at the time. I had felt the need to defend myself, to explain that I had traveled to all these European countries only because I had won fellowships and scholarships, that I never went anywhere as a child, not even in California, because my parents could not afford that. I realize now, though, I tell my friend, that even if I had been wealthy, even if I had been to Europe on a family vacation, I would never be white. No matter what my privileges amounted to, they would never add up to that. A few months after this conversation, my friend sends me a message. *I can't stop thinking about what that white dude told you in Italy*, he says. *I go from laughing to being pissed.*

I rarely allow myself to be pissed, to be angry, for very long, because angry women are not listened to. Because angry women are emotional, and they need to calm down. *Calm down, stop being paranoid, don't have a chip on your shoulder, don't victimize yourself. Be reasonable, be logical, be open, be kind, give the benefit of a doubt. You're not a black man, being shot in the streets. What is the worst thing that has happened to you? What is the worst thing that has happened to your family? Speak your trauma. Tell us how hard it is to be you. But just don't blame us. Don't blame America. America saved you. Don't blame white people. White people are saviors. Tell us your white-savior story. Tell us about the nice white people who helped you out. Who drove your mother around. Tell us about their good hearts, their good intentions. Don't tell us they were condescending. Don't tell us they exotified you, fetishized you. Don't tell us they touched your skin without your permission and thought they were paying you a compliment, thought they were being nice. They were being nice; you better believe it. Be grateful for the rides. Be grateful no one spit at you, or yelled at you, or called you slurs. Be grateful this country has come so far. Be grateful it's just curiosity, just friendliness now. Why can't you be friendly back? With a name like that, what do you expect? Of course, people need to hear it a few times, need you to spell it out, need you to tell them what it means. Some words are just more difficult for English speakers to pronounce; it's purely linguistic. Tell us how to pronounce your name in your language. Yes, your language, the one that belongs to you, the only one that is really yours. This language, English, of course, is ours.*

When my mother and her brothers and her sister were very young, my mother said, my grandmother would sometimes ask them to listen to the bullfrogs. *Can you hear them croaking?* she would ask. The bullfrogs came out to sing before and after it rained, and it rained almost every day in Rangoon, except in the dry season. The bullfrogs croaked very softly, and my mother and her siblings would have to quiet down, put away their toys, and become very still in order to hear them. They would have to move to the window, which was above the bed, and hold their breath. Eventually, they would all fall asleep for their nap.

I don't know if I ever heard the bullfrogs, my mother said. *Or if they were only in my head. I don't know if your grandmother ever heard them either.*

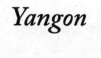

Yangon

I spent almost exactly a year, the first year of my life, in Yangon. This does not make me feel like it is where I am from. I think one should remember the place where one is from. One should have at least a single memory. Though from the nativity story of the awakened one I know that, regardless of what I remember or forget, I will always be connected to the place where I was born. I know from that story and other stories of childbirth that women return to their childhood homes to give birth to their children. The place where one is born, though it may not be the place where one is from, will always be the place where one's mother is from.

The awakened one's mother, the queen, however, did not make it back to her childhood home. She gave birth to the awakened one in a grove halfway between the palace where she lived and her parents' home where she was born. She held on to the branch of a sal tree, and as she was standing, the awakened one emerged from her right side, where a white elephant had touched her in a dream. The awakened one was thus born in an in-between place, neither his mother's home, nor his father's, but a grove of flowering trees, the flowers just blooming.

Thirty-six years after the birth and death of my brother, I asked my mother a question I had never asked her before. *What was his name?*

Not the name I had always known him by, the name my parents called him, a nickname, his home name, which I will not repeat here, outside of the home. Not the name meaning older brother, an endearment, which could even be flirtatious if used on a boy who was not actually one's older brother or cousin. Not the name my brother must have earned only after his death, since he became a big brother only after he died. Not the name my parents used to tell us about him, the older brother who would always be younger than us.

I was not asking my mother for that name, a name made up for children. I wanted to know the name my parents had given him before he died. The name they had given him at birth, the one that he was meant to carry through a long and complex life.

I am always looking for beginnings. The first that was lost, the brother I never met, the country I cannot remember. I am always looking for the moment when I can enter the stream of myself. It is not the moment of my birth, but long before that. The moment of my parents' union, their wedding held on a mythical bird floating in an artificial lake, their love that began with a borrowed book, with a handwritten letter. Or the moment of my previous death, in my great-grandfather's body, hiding in the jungle from the war. Or in a stranger's body, shot in the streets by the first soldier who pulled the first trigger.

There is often a price to pay for in-betweenness, for finding beauty and resting there, as the awakened one's mother did, and seven days after his birth, she died. With her death, the awakened one was cut off from the memory of where he was born. In Bamar, the word for womb has the word for home inside of it. The womb is our first home, and many times as a child, I used to rub my head against my mother's belly and ask if I could go back inside. She would laugh and say I got too big, I wouldn't fit anymore, and I would laugh, too, but it made me sad. There was no way home, no way back. I was blocked by my own body. Sometimes I wish I had memories of Yangon so that I could claim it. So I could say, *Yes, that is where I am from.* My sisters have memories, of my grandmother's cooking, of playing with my grandfather, of attending school. My eldest sister remembered walking to school through the woods, having to pass by the caged pigs, who scared my sister, and once she got lost and ended up spending the evening at a neighbor's house, unable to find her way home. I have heard their stories so many times it is like their memories are mine, but I know that they are not. I have no memories.

My mother said my brother's name. She said it soft and quiet, but without hesitation, as if she had been waiting all these years to say it. It was only after his name left her lips, left her body, that my mother seemed to realize that she had spoken it aloud. The spell was broken. I had finally asked the right question.

I had not known that there would be an answer, that my brother would have a different name from the one I had always known him by, that he would have a real name, a name that he was meant to use when he grew into a man. It was as if my mother only remembered this name when I asked her, as if she were surprised by the knowledge she still kept inside her. The name she had given her firstborn child. There was a sadness in her voice when she said it, but also hope. *What does it mean?* I asked, though I always resented it when strangers asked me the same question about my name. I was no stranger; I had a right to this knowledge.

In the beginning, then, there was my parents' wedding on Karaweik, a replica of a royal barge, a palatial hall shouldered by two giant birds gliding on the water. The mythical birds golden with red tails, the guardians of my mother's nightmares. My mother had not wanted an extravagant wedding; it was her father who reserved Karaweik for the reception. Only the best for his daughter, no matter the cost. The cost, my mother believed, was my brother's life.

My mother believed birds were a bad omen. She had dreams of the barge burning on the lake. A royal barge built long after the royalty was killed or exiled. Birds are terrifying because they upset the hierarchy of the universe. Lowly animals flying close to the heavens, reptilian, winged, celestial and bestial. As a child, I imagined the thirty-one planes of existence suspended above and below one another, the human realm below the celestial realms, and above the realms of animals, hungry ghosts, demons, and hells. Birds flying overhead always made me feel like I was at the bottom of the ocean.

The word for home in Bamar is the same as the word for house. Aain, a dwelling, a shelter, a residence. A hollow word, whereas home is full. Aain, like the sound of a gong, or a singing bowl struck on its side. A sound that opens, that begins. Home sounds like a mouthful, like the feeling of fullness, of bloating, homeland, expanding to cover the earth. One can fall ill from the idea of home, the idea of its loss, homesickness is felt in the body, though it arises from language. There is no abstract concept of home for the Bamar. There is a people, a land, a country, all words that evoke patriotic feelings, but home, aain, is very private, very intimate, and every house is a home, not only the house that belongs to me. Even haunted aains are someone's homes, the ghosts', perhaps, for the dead too need places to live. In English, there is no such thing as a haunted home. In this language, all ghosts are unhomed, and people without a home are ghosts.

In the beginning, there was a borrowed book, with a love letter tucked inside. So, as a child I borrowed book after book, from the school library, the public library, and the shelves of generous teachers, in search of that first book and that first letter. I never found the letter, and in its absence, I would fold myself into the books, bury myself in them. A figure of speech, to bury oneself in books, but an accurate one, for reading for me was a bit like dying. When I read, I left my body for a little while and as a ghost haunted others' lives and watched over them, even inhabited or possessed them. But maybe it was the books that possessed me, that filled my body, so that for years afterward, I was caught in this cycle of acquiring and purging my ghosts, of reading and writing, reading and writing. Dying slowly, dying bit by bit, not until I was dead, but only until I found it: the moment of my beginning, which would not be mine alone, not mine at all, which, I believed, would necessarily exclude me. A moment that took place long before my birth, and long after my death. And though I never found the love letter, I did find bookmarks, scraps of paper, receipts, grocery lists, ticket stubs, and, once, even a polaroid of a girl in the back seat of a car, staring straight into the camera.

My brother's name, my mother said, means light.

Not a burning, dazzling light, not brightness, but soft and pleasant. *Do you understand?* my mother asked. *I can't explain.*

To me, his name sounded like the word for enter, for inside, win or winn, my mother's name and my mother's father's. A light shining from the inside. A window lit up at twilight, in winter, the snow and the sky the same white-blue and the window a small glimpse of yellow, glowing softly in the quiet cold. *Clear and wide vacant space*, another translation I found of my brother's name. The space between the stars, or between the earth and the moon. The light that travels that wide expanse.

Minbu

My grandmother's golden childhood came to an end with the war. The night before her city, Minbu, was bombed, the larger city across the river, Magway, was bombed first. The people in Minbu had never seen explosions before and mistook them for fireworks. The city did not have many electric lights yet, and it was beautiful to see the night sky lit up. The river was very wide, the Irrawaddy, the lifeblood of the country, and the two cities were far enough apart, with an island between them, that the explosions were muted, and the sounds of people crying out in fear and pain did not carry across the water. In Minbu, people gathered at the riverbank and clapped.

Years later, after the war, my grandfather would sail up the same river, the Irrawaddy, which connected Gayan and Minbu, and countless other villages and towns and cities, to court my grandmother.

River is a noun derived from a verb, that which rives, which splits, rents, or severs, which tears asunder. River, splitter, renter, severer, tearer or terror. To be a river is to carve up the earth, to tear it apart, violently, with water, which has no hands. Even the sound of the word pricks the tongue. The v in the middle, which splits the word itself in two, ri and er, beginning and ending with an r, almost a palindrome. I repeat the word again and again, tasting the sharp point of the v, the suffix that follows parting my lips.

The Bamar word for river is myit. Or, the English word for myit is river. Myit, the word I learned first, meaning root or river, rhyming with pyit, the word for thick, and only one letter off from my name, in both Bamar and English. Myit, meaning deep and myint, meaning high. Bamar speakers must have known that opposites are not vastly different, but often almost the same. Like a shadow, or a reflection.

The morning after Magway was bombed, planes dropped flyers over Minbu. They were going to be bombed that night. The story my father told was not of my grandmother, who made it safely to the beach, which was the designated evacuation site, but of her relative, an uncle, who had forgotten something back at his house. He told his wife he would catch up with her at the beach, but he never showed. When the bombings ended and they returned to the city the next day, they found the uncle's body blown apart at the threshold of his house.

My grandmother's mother died during the war, when the family was hiding in the countryside. I asked my father what she died of, and he said, *she was a very fragile sort of person.* It was said she died because she could not endure the fright and shock of the war. *But it's hard to say,* my father said, *in those days, during the war, they couldn't take her to see a good doctor.*

My other grandmother, my mother's mother, had also lost a parent during the war, when she was about the same age. For a long time, I thought it was a strange coincidence that both my grandmothers would have suffered the same fate. Both great-grandparents were in their early forties when they passed away, and both grandmothers were teenagers. It was only later that I realized it was not a coincidence at all, but simply a common fate for many families.

The British invaded through the rivers, through the myit, which they renamed river. The roots of the country became that which tore the country apart, that which split, rent, and severed the land. The British sailed up the Irrawaddy with their Trojan horse of a fleet, with their decoy prince, and the people lined up along the banks to watch it pass. In Bamar, the words for invasion, conquest, and occupation are everyday words, the same words I used as a child while playing. To invade is to butt in, to conquer is to boss, and to occupy is to hog. I do not know if the Bamar words were meant to soften the shame of being colonized, of falling for a mean trick, or if it is the English words, our euphemisms, that allow English-speaking children to grow up and colonize others without shame.

If the English word for river had not been river, but had been something else, root, for example, or depth, I think the British would have sailed up the Irrawaddy all the same. Roots too can be parasitic. There are plants that extract nutrients and water, not from the earth, but from the bodies of other plants. There is a name for roots that do this: haustoria. There is a name for every kind of violence.

I never asked my grandmother about how the war affected her, except once when she was already losing her memory. We were seated at the dining table at my aunt's house. My father, me, and my two aunts who lived with my grandmother. My grandmother acted as if she did not hear my question. Maybe she did not, or maybe she did not want to answer. My father and my aunts filled her silence with their own stories.

At the end of her life, my grandmother no longer recognized me. The last time she spoke to me, she said, *Who is this child? Who is this pretty child?* I did not know how to answer her. *It's me*, I kept saying. *Don't you remember? It's me.* But my grandmother did not remember. She could not even remember her own children.

My grandmother had seven children who lived. Three boys and four girls. I remember hearing once, as a child, that she had had as many as a dozen pregnancies. She had spent over two decades bearing and birthing children. My youngest aunt, who was a decade younger than my father, said it was because my grandfather loved children so much he always wanted to have more. I wonder at what point a woman begins to lose herself to her children. At what point her body is created from them, by them, rather than the other way around.

After the war, after my grandmother's mother passed away, my grandmother's father married his mistress. I cannot imagine that either my grandmother or the mistress could have been too happy with this arrangement. My grandmother, my father said, married my grandfather young so she could escape her new stepmother.

My grandmother and grandfather were half first cousins. My grandfather's father and my grandmother's mother were half brother and sister. The two that died young. The two from the family that lost all their land. My great-grandmother's older sister, who had played matchmaker for my grandmother's parents, was the same woman whose husband gambled away their family's land. Because my grandmother grew up in Minbu, in the north, and my grandfather grew up in Gayan, which was in the south, almost by the ocean, they did not see much of each other growing up. The one time my grandmother visited Minbu as a child, my grandfather, who was older by a few years, made her cry when he stole her snack and ate it. *He received a good spanking for that*, my father said, laughing.

Right before the war broke out, during the Japanese occupation, the grandfather that my grandparents shared was dying, and my grandmother and her mother returned to Gayan to be with him during his final days. My grandfather had also returned to Gayan from Rangoon, though he had not yet joined the independence army, not yet left for the mountains. My great-great-grandfather took a few months to die, and during that time, my grandmother and grandfather got to know each other, for the first time, as teenagers. I do not know what was exchanged between them during this liminal time, this time of suspended death and imminent war, but a few years later, after the war, my grandfather sailed up and down the Irrawaddy to court my grandmother, and soon, they were married.

When I was young, I used to think about all the babies my grandparents had who did not live. I asked my mother once why they did not live, and she said she did not know. My mother said, *in those days, right after the war, many babies died.*

I have an image in my head of a baby drowning in a shallow tub. Not the built-in, porcelain-enameled kind found in American homes, but a large steel basin, used for collecting rainwater. The baby is one of my grandmother's babies who died. It is dying now. I see its little head slide under the water. I see it but no one else does. I do not know if my mother said one of the babies drowned, or if I imagined it all on my own. I see the baby drowning, dying, and I think I understand my grandmother better, her timidity, her distrust, the way she held her lips or her shoulders, tightly, like she had something to protect.

Providence

In the beginning, there was a train to Boston. This was the first day she felt grown up, riding a train on her own, and being the first day, the feeling was still wonderful. She looked out the window, the white beech trees floated by, trees unlike any she had ever seen, cold unlike any she had ever felt, and the song she was listening to, the moment existing inside of that song, unending as well, and she thought she would always be eighteen and it would always be autumn, before the first real winter of her life.

On the ride back from Boston, the woman driving them, who would kill herself a few years later, said the glowing night sky was just a remnant of summer. At this latitude, the woman said, the autumn sky always had a touch of orange. She sat in the back seat in the darkness. It was September, the first of the ember months. Walking across the main green later that night, or another night that week, that year, or the next, she looked up at the sky, framed by the trees and the slanting roof of Sayles Hall. There were no stars, no moon, only a thick layer of clouds, opaque and absolute.

The first time it snowed that winter, the first real winter of her life, she nearly slept through it. She had stayed up the night before to write a paper. Her phone rang and she turned it off. There were knocks on the door and she ignored them. She was a heavy sleeper. Finally, her roommate returned to wake her up. The roommate opened the curtains she had shut and said, *look*. She looked up from the bed. It was snowing. She went to the window. The red brick sidewalks were speckled with white, Charlesfield Street gleaming black with wet. She looked at the telephone lines and tried to catch the moment when the snow crossed them. She could not see it. She went back to sleep that day, but it became a habit of hers to sit by a window, usually late at night, and watch the snow fall. Snow, which her ancestors had never seen, she thought, though it soon occurred to her that probably her earliest ancestors had seen it, the ones who descended from the north, who crossed the Himalayas and endured the cold and ice, for the promise of a fertile valley.

She, too, had traveled far, across an entire continent, of which she had seen very little, for the promise of the new, the unknown. A place that no one she knew had ever been to, a place that would be hers alone. The name of the city itself sounded like a promise—*Providence*, in the foreknowing and care of God. On a run with a friend one evening, she remembered looking into the lighted windows of professors' homes and feeling nostalgic for a childhood she had never had, which she glimpsed inside of these homes. Family dinners around a large mahogany table, a fireplace, bookshelves lined with history. She was always looking into or out of windows, separated from the world by her own reflection.

Sometimes, it even felt as if she were looking into her own window, her own life, which she could not enter. She loved, and her love was unrequited. Their hands knocked together when they walked but his never grasped hers. She was always standing at a threshold, to his room or his building, the heavy door held open by his body, though she too could feel its weight. One night under the portico, he had said, *The highway sounds like the ocean*, and she had held her breath to listen. She could not hear what he heard, but the shadow of trees danced against the brick wall of his building and they made her feel underwater.

In the bathroom of an organization where she worked one summer, an organization that had been founded by queer youth a decade ago to oppose deportations and racial profiling in the city, there was a quotation taped to the bathroom wall that read, *Rather than falling in love we must learn to stand in love.* The quotation was attributed to a Buddhist monk she had never heard of. She had always disliked the phrase *to fall in love.* She did not even know if an equivalent phrase existed in Bamar. When her parents told her stories about their court-ship, they used the word kyait, like, when talking about the past, and chit, love, when talking about the present. They never explained the moment when words and feelings changed.

The summer she worked at the political action queer alliance, she and her unrequited love went on two long walks to the Steel Yard. She went to buy a bicycle and he accompanied her so he could interview the Marxists and anarchists who worked there. He was writing a thesis on anarchist movements in the United States, the only development studies major to focus his research on a so-called developed country. The Steel Yard was two miles from campus and he walked his bike the entire way so they could ride back together. A boy walking his bike so he could walk with her. The most romantic gesture she could think of at the time. In her memory, the two visits to the Steel Yard blend together. She tried to pay a Marxist and he threw up his hands. The mechanic working on the bike she chose called her a woman, which no one had ever done before. Both times, her bike was not ready, and they had to walk all the way back to campus. She cannot remember the third trip she must have made to the Steel Yard, when she was finally able to pick up her bike. Did she ride back alone, under the highway overpass and across the river, helmetless on streets with no bike lanes? She cannot imagine it, but she cannot imagine walking her bike, either, the entire two miles back to campus. She did not possess his patience.

Her unrequited love's mother was born in the same part of the world where she was born and had moved to this country at the same age she had. When they discovered this fact, her unrequited love had lit up, and she felt or imagined some of his tenderness for his mother transfer onto her. First generation, second generation. She was his past and he was her future, though what she wanted was to be his future. What she wanted was to reenact her parents' courtship. Meet at eighteen, borrow books, exchange love letters. She was eighteen when she met her unrequited love, and so was he. Their birthdays only one day apart, though given the difference in time zones, it was likely they had been born at the same time. They did not borrow books, but on their shared birthday, they would gift them to each other. Or maybe this happened only one year. There is only one book on her shelf, a slender volume with a blank white sky on the cover, that she is certain she received from him. The summer she traveled to the country where she was born and he traveled to the country where his mother was born, they had exchanged emails, despite not having regular access to the internet in the so-called developing world. She wrote to him from internet cafes, or the homes of well-to-do distant relatives. The emails were not the love letters her parents had written during their courtship, though she had thought they would one day be precious.

Years later, when she is teaching creative writing to undergraduates, she is amused by how many of her students' stories are about first love, and how many of them are touchingly bad. Her unrequited love's lasting gift to her, she thinks, is that he did not allow her to write a love story. Their story was not a story about love. It was not a story at all. There was nothing that was theirs, only what was hers. The city's twilight, the streets washed in lamplight, in rain or ice. Storm drains and the sound of water falling darkly into the sewers. She loved not him exactly, but the absence of him, the distance of him. Walking back to her dorm alone after saying goodnight or watching him onstage from the back of the crowd. This did not mean it had nothing to do with him, because it did. It could not have happened with anybody else. It: the coming into herself, the beginning of herself. Out of all the books she read in college, used or library copies, there was only one in which she recognized herself. A translation from the modern Greek, a novel about a young woman who joins the underground resistance and falls in love. Or maybe it was the other way around, the young woman joins the resistance because she falls in love. There was a line she memorized from the book. A question. *I used to think of him in the prison yard, with the bitter taste in his mouth . . . his loneliness at night . . . But when it came down to it, who thought in that way of me?* The first real winter of her life was followed by the first real spring. The falling snow turned to rain before it landed, the ice melted in the river, and the magnolias bloomed. Spring became her favorite season in the city. At the earliest sign of warmth, she and everyone around her would bare their bodies—arms and legs, shoulders, throat, and feet. Gooseflesh covered their exposed skin but none of them felt cold. It was springtime, when the whole world was budding, when she biked in the rain with a plastic bag over the seat, biked in a dress, not caring who saw her underwear. She was safe. She had arrived. She no longer had to explain herself: presence, body, or name. When she began writing again, no one told her to *write about her country and her people*, no one told her to *use her gift, her talent*. Talent was a public-school word, she learned, it only had meaning in places where it was rare, remarkable. At her private university, where she was accumulating tens of thousands of dollars in loans, it was presumed, but also questioned, deemed "problematic" and irrelevant, like all her other lower-middle-class beliefs and values. Integrity, humility, fairness. She wanted an education so she could help others, so she could make a difference, give back, all the clichés. But the more she learned about the world, the less she wanted to be any part of it. All she could do was watch the snow fall, the rain, listen to a storm drain, a distant highway, notice the way the sky changed colors. She wrote all of this down, which preserved it somehow, a small part of it, made glossy and hard under the tip of her pen.

Sittwe

Sittwe, in both Bamar and Rakhine, means where war meets, or where one meets war. Where two parties meet in war. Twe, to meet or to encounter, but also to see, to sight, to glimpse. To see war coming, by land and by sea, and to meet it. Sittwe, where war was sighted and where war was fought. A city born from the battlefield, a memorial for the dead. The Rakhine believed that all who fought in the war against the Bamar died. A war without survivors, a city that was never a city until it was lost.

After the military coup in September, the second in my parents' young life, universities and colleges slowly reopened, and my parents were asked to return to Sittwe. My father turned thirty-one just a day after martial law was established. My mother's birthday was a few months later, at the end of November. By then, my father had flown back to Sittwe, and my mother had moved back in with her parents in Bauk Htaw. In the second trimester of being pregnant with me, my mother had begun to bleed. Her condition was called a threatened abortion. The doctors prescribed bed rest, so my mother submitted a medical leave to Sittwe Degree College and stayed behind in Rangoon with my sisters.

In the months my mother spent lying in bed pregnant with me, the new military government, which called itself SLORC, the State Law and Order Restoration Council, washed all the temples and pagodas in the city. To cleanse the country. To prepare for a new beginning. It was to cover the evidence of their slaughter. The bloodstains on the temple walls and floors.

My parents had one year left of their term in Sittwe, but after what happened in the aftermath of 8888, what they had lived through, they were not planning to do another three-year term, in Sittwe or anywhere else in the country. My mother's dream to go abroad became my family's dream, or, rather, their urgent plan.

My father began applying for teaching jobs abroad, and as soon as her period of prescribed bed rest was over, my mother spent all her time in Rangoon lobbying for my father and her to be transferred back to the capital. She figured they would find more opportunities to go abroad in Rangoon than in Sittwe. When her medical leave expired, my mother submitted maternity leave, and managed to stay in Rangoon for the duration of her pregnancy. She returned to Sittwe only after I was born, for her duty report at Sittwe Degree College, a bureaucratic formality that needed to be observed in order for her to be transferred elsewhere.

My mother left me in Rangoon for two weeks with her parents when she returned to Sittwe for her duty report. She said soon after I was born, her uncle invited an astrologer to divine my fate, and this person had told my mother that I should never be brought to Sittwe. I was a lucky child, my mother said the astrologer said, but I would lose all my powers if I was taken to Sittwe. If I stayed in Rangoon, however, I would be able to bring both my parents back to me.

My mother believed the astrologer. She believed that I had magical powers, that I was a child gifted by weikzas, a child that had been promised to her in a dream. So I was left behind in Rangoon, for my own protection. When my mother returned from Sittwe, weeks or perhaps only days later, there was a letter waiting for her. A letter addressed to my father from a university in Bangkok. The thing she had been waiting for all these years.

In June of 1990, a week after my birth, SLORC changed all the names in the country. Burma became Myanmar and Rangoon became Yangon. In 1962, when the first military junta took power, they too had changed the country's name, from the post-independence Union of Burma to the Socialist Republic of the Union of Burma. In 1990, the second military junta changed the name again to Union of Myanmar. They claimed that Myanmar was a more inclusive term than Burma, which translated to land of the Bamar, but Bamar and Myanmar were synonyms, so Myanmar also translated to land of the Bamar. There is no word, no name that unites all the people who lived or live in the region now encompassed by the boundaries of the present-day country. Like a human body, the region's boundaries had always been ambiguous, always changing. The Bamar themselves recognized that we were not indigenous to the land, that once, we too had come from elsewhere, from abroad, from outside. The word for ethnic minority in Bamar is taing yin thar, which means native, aboriginal, or indigenous. Minority is implied. To be ethnic was to be marked and marginalized, but also to be more of a native in Burma, the land of the Bamar, than the Bamar themselves.

My father received an offer to teach at a university in Thailand. Normally, schools did not hire instructors without an in-person interview, but the person who wrote my father's offer letter was going on sabbatical and wanted to expedite the hiring process, so he bent some rules. My mother said this was fortuitous because my father would have never left the country without a job offer. *You know how he is*, my mother said, and I knew because I was the same: cautious, anxious, resistant to change.

Even with the job offer, my parents could not leave the country for several more months. In August of 1989, they were transferred back to Rangoon, now spelled Yangon, and asked to work through the end of the year. It was only in January of 1990 that my father finally left for Bangkok. I do not know if he knew then that he would never come back. I think he must have known. My father always liked to say, *I never look back*, in a silly voice, as if he were a tough guy in an action movie, but I think he meant it. In July of 1990, my mother followed him with three children in tow. My eldest sister was six, my middle sister was about to turn four, and I had just turned one.

When my parents speak about Burma, they still use the old, pre-1990 names. The British were remarkably—if not maliciously—bad at transliterating Bamar words, but my parents still said *Rangoon* instead of Yangon, *Prome* instead of Pyay, and *Tenasserim* instead of Tanintharyi. When my parents speak in Bamar, they pronounce these names properly, but whenever they switch to English, they return to these British misnomers out of habit. When I was older, I learned that many Western countries, including the United States, used the country's old name, Burma, as a way to not acknowledge the legitimacy of the military junta. I wondered if it was also possible to not acknowledge the legitimacy of British colonialism. I had always resented having to identify with *Burma*, *Burman*, and *Burmese*, when all of these were anglicized names. *Bamar* was what I identified with, what united my family with other immigrants and refugees, regardless of race, or ethnicity, or religion. It was only when I returned to Yangon to teach English one summer in college that I heard the word Myanmar used as an identity marker. *We are Myanmar*, my teenage students said. It was one of the few phrases they had been taught in English. Myanmar, a nationality. Something from which those of us who grew up in the diaspora had been excluded.

In my first-grade Burmese textbook, there was a map of Myanmar and its seven states and seven regions. Each of the states was marked by a cute cartoon couple dressed in traditional ethnic garb. Above Kachin State was a Kachin couple, the girl bedecked in a cylindrical headdress and the boy in a head wrap; above Kayah State was a Kayah couple, the girl wearing a one-shoulder dress and the boy wearing trousers; above Kayin State was a Kayin couple, the boy and girl both wearing the boxy tunics I recognized because my aunt Stella was Kayin and had once gifted us these tunics for Christmas. Above Chin State was a Chin couple, above Mon State a Mon couple, above Shan State a Shan couple, and above Rakhine State a Rakhine couple.

There was no Bamar State. Instead, the Bamar couple was positioned above the seven divisions, Irrawaddy, Bago, Magway, Mandalay, Sagaing, Tanintharyi, and Yangon. The Bamar girl was wearing a htamein with a blouse and shawl, her hair in a half bun, and the boy was in a paso and a collarless jacket. All the couples on the map looked identical except for their dress.

On one of the twenty-two trips my mother took between Sittwe and Rangoon, her plane got caught in a storm. My mother was traveling alone with my middle sister, who she remembered was bouncing in her lap, before falling asleep on her, *like a little monkey.* Just as the plane was about to begin its descent to Sittwe, there was an announcement from the cockpit. Due to the bad weather, the pilots could not find the island. To make matters worse, the plane did not have enough fuel to fly back to Rangoon, so the crew had no choice but to fly in circles and hope that they caught a glimpse of land. When the announcement ended, the lights in the cabin began to flicker. *It was like a movie*, my mother said. *The plane was jumping up and down, everyone was panicking, crying out, my knees were shaking.* My mother thought she was going to die. After some time, a second announcement came on. The pilot said they were almost out of fuel, so they had no choice but to guess where Sittwe was and land the plane blindly. The storm had reduced visibility to almost zero. *My heart and my intestines were flipped upside down*, my mother said, *my whole chest was frozen with fear.* As the plane descended, my mother said all the prayers she knew, dredged up some courage, and prepared to die well. Then, finally, she heard the wheels touch down on asphalt, on solid land. Outside, the storm was still raging, the heavy rain and wind pounding against her small plastic window, but she knew she had made it, she was still alive.

V

Years and years later, she is sitting in a bookstore in a small town where she lives, listening to a best-selling author tell a story about the author's immigration experience. The bookstore is overcrowded. Every foldout chair is occupied, and people are standing at the peripheries, between aisles of books, or sitting cross-legged on the floor at the author's feet. The author is telling a story about the flight from the country of the author's birth to this country, where the author now lives. The story is linear. The plane flies straight from one country to the other. When the author shares a humorous detail, the audience laughs; when the author sighs, the audience makes sympathetic noises. She is silent. Sitting in the small foldout chair, surrounded by the bodies of strangers, she feels a dull panic unfurling inside her. It is the same feeling she used to get when as a small child she lost track of her mother at a grocery store or the mall. The feeling of being lost. She realizes that she cannot remember her "immigration experience." Or, in her case, her immigration experiences. She cannot remember the flight she took as a baby from the country of her birth, and she cannot remember the flight she took as a young child from the country where she formed her first memories. She and the best-selling author were the same age when they arrived in this country, but unlike the author, she has no story to tell an audience. No details, no outline, not even a trace. She should have been old enough to remember. She has clear memories of times when she was much younger: the time she fell down the stairs or the time their neighbor's dog gave birth to puppies. The author is reading from the author's book now, but she is not listening. She is trying to remember. A flight from Bangkok to San Francisco. A long flight, a full day and night of travel. They were sitting in the middle aisle of the plane, she thinks, but maybe not all five of them, maybe her family was separated, her mother and one sister sitting apart. She was beside her father, she thinks, or maybe it was her mother, maybe they were all together. She is not remembering, she knows, but guessing, inventing. She tries to picture their airplane moving through the sky, crossing the Pacific Ocean, but there is a hole in the sky where the plane should be. The hole is an entrance to a tunnel, she thinks, a tunnel of nothing that swallowed the plane. She read in a book that her friend wrote about the death of her friend's mother that memories are precarious. Each time a memory is recalled, it must be pieced together again as if for the first time. Another friend once told her that he knew a man who believed he was an angel before he was born. This man could not remember having been an angel anymore, but he could still remember the feeling of remembering that he was. She treasured that: a memory of a memory. She had always been fascinated by traces: the morning frost on the school field, dreams, old photographs, the fog that sometimes settled over the valley, seashells, fruit peels, lost teeth. Her middle sister had collected all their baby teeth in an old pencil sharpener. She doesn't know where it is anymore, but she can still picture it: a little pink rectangle that slid open like a matchbox. She wonders if it would have been easier to remember her story if her story had been simpler. An immigrant is a person who is born in one country and goes to live in another country. She was born in one country, lived in another country, and then lived some more in yet another country. Does that make her a double immigrant, then? She does not like the word "immigrant" to describe herself. The word is too active, too evocative of movement and agency. She did not go from one country to another. She was brought along. When she was thirteen months old, her mother carried her onto a plane and left the country where she was born. Her mother said she cried the whole way, on the plane, at the airport. Her mother said she didn't stop crying even when they finally arrived at their new home, a small townhouse on a dead-end street, which would become the first home she could remember. When she was seven and three-quarters, her mother and father led her onto another plane that brought her to this country. Her mother said she did not cry then, and since she cannot remember the flight, she has to believe what her mother said.

What she does remember is crying every morning she woke up at her aunt's house. They lived with her aunt and her grandparents when they first arrived in this country, in a low, one-story house with three bedrooms, one bathroom, and a large tree in the front yard. One bedroom was occupied by her aunt, another by her grand-parents, and the third, which had been her uncle's room, was set aside for her family. She remembers that the room still smelled like her uncle, cigarettes and leather, and something else that only years later she would come to recognize as the smell of alcohol. The room also still contained his things—model airplanes, helicopters, and cars. She did not know why her uncle collected toys when he was an adult. She did not know where he slept after they moved into his room and nobody told her. She did not know where her aunt slept every night either. It seemed to her that the only permanent residents of the house were her grandparents. Her grandfather, her grandmother, and now her mother, her eldest sister, her middle sister, and herself. Her father returned to Bangkok to finish his PhD. Her father had been working on his PhD for as long as she could remember, and she knew what the letters stood for. Doctor of philosophy, a terminal degree. She was afraid of doctors and terminal illnesses, but she liked the sound of philosophy. It had the word soft inside of it, and ended the way it began, with a gentle puff of air escaping the lips. Maybe she cried every morning because she missed her father, or because she missed her former home, or because she had no friends at her new school. She cannot remember the reason. Maybe there was no reason, or none that she could name, either now, or back then as a child. All she remembers is waking up and crying, or waking up to find herself already crying, her face wet with tears and a sob in her throat. Her mother and her aunt and her grand-mother did everything they could to calm her, but she only cried harder. She did not stop. Then one day, her mother made her stop. One day, in the dark hallway of her aunt's house, her mother knelt down before her and said, it is bad luck to cry when nothing bad has happened, when nobody has died. *Do you want something bad to happen?* her mother asked. *Do you want your mother or your father to die?* And she did not. She did not want her parents to die, ever, and the thought that she had nearly killed them, accidentally, with her bad-luck tears, was so horrible and so painful that it changed something inside her. She stopped crying, that morning and every morning afterward, for months, maybe even for years.

Or maybe she didn't stop crying, but she stopped occupying her body more than necessary, so she could no longer tell if she was cry-ing or not, and years later, walking back from the reading with her husband and her colleague, defending Virginia Woolf, whom she felt the best-selling author had slighted, she cannot remember either crying or not crying. Her memories of the time at her aunt's house are all in the third person. She sees a girl sitting on the edge of a futon in the family room, her face bloated and red, her mouth fail-ing to form words. She sees her aunt and her grandmother standing in the kitchen, their mouths sharp and forceful, their eyes the same. Her aunt cuts through the air with her arm, pointing with her whole hand. Look at this mess, she seems to say, though the scene is muted in her memory, though she cannot hear her aunt's raised voice. Not the aunt whom the house belonged to, but the older aunt, who had come to visit, or rather to inspect them. And they had failed the in-spection. The woman crying in the living room behind the kitchen. The girl on the futon. Another girl standing with a broom in her hand, trying to clean up, to make it better. Maybe she is the girl crying, she thinks, or the girl trying to clean, or maybe the two girls are her sisters, and she is the one who is missing from the memory. If there had been a mirror at the end of the living room, behind her mother, maybe she would have seen herself in the scene, across three rooms, all connected the way she later came to learn only houses in California were. When she lived in Madrid, she used to walk to the Prado and stand before Velázquez's *Las Meninas*, which she had seen for the first time in her Spanish textbook. Back in high school, she had stared and stared at the small dark rectangle in her textbook and had been haunted by the image of the king and queen reflected in the mirror in the murky background of the painting. She was not afraid to look at the dead. She knew that Velázquez and la infanta and las meninas were all long dead, she had even gone to the royal crypts, but it was terrible to stand in the place of the dead, to stand before the painting, which was so much larger than the little rectangle she had cherished in high school, and stand before a painted mirror that reflected not her own face but the faces of the dead. She knows she was not dead as a child in her aunt's house, but without a mirror in her memory, something to reflect herself back to her, she is not sure if she was alive. In another memory, she and her middle sister are taking a bubble bath. In their former home, there had been no flush toilets and no bathtubs or showers. They washed with a showerhead attached to a faucet, or with plastic buckets. Baths were a luxury available once a year when they stayed at a high-rise hotel on the beach, a vacation paid for by the university where their parents worked. Now, at their aunt's house, she and her sisters could take a bath whenever they wanted and for as long as they wanted, if their mother was not there. She cannot remember where their mother was that day. At work, probably, at one of her many jobs, day care worker, cashier, substitute teacher's aide. She cannot remember where her eldest sister or her grandmother or her aunt were either. It was just her and her middle sister, splashing each other with the bathwater gone cold, the bubbles gone flat. She felt guilty and afraid even before their grandfather began pounding at the door. He was yelling something as well, but she could not make it out. She only felt the sound reverberate through her body and the gray water that contained it. In her memory, she is both inside the tub, and outside the bathroom door, she is both herself and her grandfather. When the door between them cracks open, she sees both horrors: two skinny naked children, shivering, and a rimy old man, blind in one eye. She can feel both the shame of being seen and the shame of seeing.

In the days, weeks, and months that followed the best-selling author's reading, she tries to gather her memories, to collect them, the same way her middle sister had collected their baby teeth in the pencil sharpener. Her father had encouraged her sister's collection, not only of teeth, but of magnets, seashells, and other junk. Her father had said the urge to collect things was a mark of genius, the urge to give order to a disparate and divergent world, to find patterns, to complete a set. Her father collected stamps. Whenever he received a letter in the mail, he would rip off the corner with the stamp and place it in a bowl of water. When she was old enough, her father would let her peel the wet stamps off the wet paper. She had to be very careful, to pull slowly but steadily or else she would rip the stamp in half. Despite her best efforts, she often ripped the stamps anyway, in half, or in shreds, sometimes leaving a corner behind. Her father never scolded her, never got upset. Recalling her memories now was like peeling those soggy stamps as a child. She had to be very careful, to work slowly, but not too slowly, and to apply just the right amount of pressure. If she pulled too slowly, the memories ripped in half, and she lost them before she could remember in full. If she pulled too fast or too hard, she was left with only a trace, a strip, or a corner of the memories. She sat in her office with its bare bookshelves and cavernous ceilings, or sat at her desk in her bedroom, a thin white curtain separating her from the parking lot and the street beyond, and submerged herself into the bowl of water sticky with the residue of glue. It was only in this water that patterns began to come loose and emerge. She learned, for example, that she had two discrete sets of memories. Memories of school, and memories of home, or more accurately of homelessness. She does not know if she has a right to that word, if it is a matter of rights, of right and wrong, but it is the only word that she knows for the time at her aunt's house and the time after they were kicked out of her aunt's house. *Kicked out* is what she has always said to herself. She cannot remember actually ever saying it aloud, *we were kicked out, my mother and my sisters and I.* Perhaps someone else had said it aloud, her eldest sister. It sounds like something her sister would say. Flippant and bitter. It sounds like her sister, but she cannot hear her sister's voice. She cannot hear any voices speaking of what happened. No one spoke of it in her family. It was another blank space in her memory, another tunnel of nothing that she had to crawl through on her hands and knees to emerge on the other side: in another bathroom, in another woman's house. The woman is not an aunt, is not a relation in any way, is hardly even a friend of her mother's. They are guests at the woman's apartment, more so than they were at her aunt's house. The situation is precarious. She does not like the woman's broad face, does not trust her, but the woman tells her to take a bath, to enjoy it, to take as long as she wants, so she sits in the clean, white tub while her mother and the woman talk in the living room. It is only now, as an adult, that she realizes that the baths had been used to distract her, to appease her, the warm water like a sedative, a drug, so she would not ask questions, so she would not cry and make a scene. Maybe, she thinks, this is why she has never been able to enjoy a bath, even though she tried many times, knowing that it was one of the few pleasures allowed to women. Once, she had lit candles and incenses and poured out a jar of bath salts, but after only a few minutes in the tub, she convinced herself that her bathroom was haunted. She realizes now that she was right, the bathroom in her old apartment had been haunted, though not by a ghost as she thought. It had been haunted by her. One can be a ghost while one is still alive, she thinks, if one carries what one cannot remember. Empty memories, blank memories, absent memories. The empty but occupied space inside of her was a breeding ground for ghosts. Her middle sister believed that empty spaces invited ghosts to fill them: basements, attics, closets, stairwells, the space underneath a bed. As children, she and her middle sister slept together in the same bed, and they had a bedtime ritual of tucking their blankets underneath their feet. They did not tuck the blankets under the mattress—the boogeyman could have easily pulled them out that way. They tucked the blankets around their feet and underneath their legs. It was only when she felt her lower body wrapped tightly in this way that she felt safe. The boogeyman, she knows now, was also a ghost conjured by fear. They could not name what they feared, she and her sister, but they could name him: a boogeyman who lived under their bed. She did not remember feeling afraid at her aunt's house, or in the places where they lived afterward, places she can hardly remember. The fear came only later, after she and her family found their own place to live. Or maybe the fear was always there, but it surfaced only after it was safe enough, when it knew that she could manage it—by tucking in her blankets, by avoiding baths. Lately, she has been hearing a ringing in her right ear. A buzzing, as if an animal were trapped inside, or as if she were hearing the sound of her own blood pounding. It is loudest when she awakes from a nightmare, or when she is working late at night, still at her desk while her husband is already in bed, or already asleep. The categories of illness baffle her. It is not a mark of mental illness to hear a buzzing that others cannot, but it is a mark of mental illness to hear

voices that others cannot. The sound in her ears, she thinks, however, is a voice. The voice of the memories she cannot recall strain-
ing to be heard, which is why the sound fills her with panic, with
the fear of drowning. She will drown in this blood in her ears, she
thinks, in this water of stamp residue.

Her memories of school are clearer. At school, she had her own
cubby and her own desk, where she could keep her things. She
remembers clearly her plastic pink Barbie backpack and her red-
white-and-blue tracksuit, which she knows she also wore on the
flight she took to the United States. She knows this only because
there is a photograph of her and her sisters posing at an airport in
their brand-new clothes. Maybe the picture was taken at the airport in Bangkok or the airport on their layover, if they had a layover. She does not think it was taken at the San Francisco airport.
When she looks at the photograph, she is surprised by how big
she looks. A seven-year-old turning eight in three months. It is
incredible to her how little she can remember of that time. She remembers the first rainy day in the second grade. They had recess
indoors, and she wanted to play with the Lincoln Logs, which, it
turned out, was a toy reserved for boys. Two boys did not want to
share the logs with her, but a third came to her defense. *How would
you feel if you were in a new country and you didn't have any friends
yet and you didn't speak the language?* The boy had said all of that. A
whole speech. The only thing was, she did speak the language, had
been speaking it since she began speaking at all, but she did not tell
this boy because she did not speak to boys.

There were other times at school, however, when no one defended
her, when she was alone. The time her whole third-grade class laughed
out loud because she could not correctly punctuate a date, could not
understand why a comma needed to separate the month and the year,

but not the month and the day. Even as a child, she had a strong sense of justice and felt it was unfair that only some things had to be cordoned off, excluded. Everyone or no one deserved to be loved. Then there was the time her classmate stole her and her sister's entire collection of stickers, which the three of them had spent several months curating, through strategic trades and acquisitions. She had begged her sisters to let her bring the stickers to school with her, to show off to her classmates, and though it was their most precious possession and she was just a third grader, finally her sisters relented. It was a glorious day. With the sticker book in hand, she transformed into a real girl, even with her bowl haircut and her hand-me-down clothes, her foreignness and her strange homeschool manners. The other girls spoke to her for the first time, laughed with her, invited her to join their games. She was so drunk with happiness she was careless. She did not watch over her Barbie backpack and the book of stickers inside. She did not notice how one girl kept her occupied on the playground while the other girls performed the heist. Even when she returned from school that day, empty-handed, inconsolable, she did not know what had happened, how she lost the stickers. Her sisters had to explain it to her. *Don't ever trust anyone*, they had said. And she knew what they meant by that: don't trust anyone *else*, anyone who was not in their immediate family. So, for the rest of the year that she and her middle sister were at the same elementary school, she followed her sister everywhere. To her sister's immense credit, despite being a full three grades ahead, she allowed it. She knows now what it must have cost her sister socially, to be seen with a third grader, but at the time, she did not understand what her sister had done for her sake. Unlike her, her sister was a beautiful child. She could have made friends. Because of her, however, her sister's only friend was a girl whose four younger brothers also followed her around. She did not know how she knew this, but her sister's friend's family, like hers, was different. They dressed as if they belonged to a different time, or place, or perhaps it was something more abstract, like a different religion, or different politics. At the end of her sister's time at elementary school, the friend's family had to move away. She did not know why, but she knew it was not their choice. She has a clear memory of saying goodbye to them, the two parents, her sister's friend, and her four younger brothers, all piled into a single car already packed with their things. The older she gets, the further she gets from this memory, the more she is convinced the memory is not a memory at all, but something she imagined. A goodbye she had created to fill the absence of a goodbye. The only thing that she remembers for certain is her mother saying it is bad luck to have a daughter and four sons. That was exactly how many children were needed for a funeral, a daughter to cry, and four sons to bear the coffin. Her sister's friend left, as if in a funeral procession, and so did all the friends she managed to make in the years that followed. They moved away, to Stockton, to Sacramento, to cities in Colorado. It only occurred to her, years later, when she herself moved to Denver for graduate school, that her friends' families had left the valley because they could no longer afford to live there. In Colorado, Californians were resented, were held responsible for rising home prices and the cost of living. Once, a bouncer at a bar jokingly denied her entry on account of her California driver's license. *It isn't our fault*, she wanted to say to him. All her friends moved away because, like her, their parents did not make much money. As a child, she did not know how to guess how much money her classmates' parents made. She could not tell the difference between her clothes and theirs, her things and theirs. But most of the other children could already discriminate, and they avoided her like her poorness might be contagious. So, unlike most children, she loved class and hated recess. Those fifteen minutes when she was released into the playground were agony. She would walk slowly from the restroom to the water fountain and back and forth to fill the time.

Soon, the other children caught on to what she was doing, and she had to change tactics. She took to walking briskly all over the school, from the library to the restroom, to one end of the playground and back to the water fountain. She found that if she walked quickly and with a sense of purpose, she became nearly invisible. Everyone assumed that she had somewhere to be, that she belonged. At dinner one night, while helping her brainstorm for a job interview, her husband remarks that the movement in her novel is interesting because it is pointless. *The book is about movement itself,* he says. *It's about process and not the end goal.* She immediately and categorically rejects his interpretation, begins listing all of her characters' motivations and desires. *You are wrong,* she wants to say, but she knows he is not, she knows that he saw, like he always did, the assumptions and experiences underlying her most opaque and lyrical work. She writes in the same way she got through recess, by creating arbitrary goals, excuses to move from one place to another, moving in circles, the movement itself an approximation of living, a mimicry of life. Someone else once said to her that the spaces one learns to navigate as a child stay with one for the rest of one's life. This idea terrified her. She thought of the small, poorly lit, and eclectically furnished spaces she lived in growing up. Was she doomed to move through such dark and cluttered spaces for the rest of her life? Crawling up the stairs on all fours, hiding in the narrow space between the back of the couch and the bookshelf, locking herself in the only bathroom for a bit of privacy, walking out in the cold to do laundry. Once her family moved into a condominium with a washer and dryer in the unit, laundry became her favorite chore. Her mother would jokingly remind her not to put her parents in the wash too because she was in the habit of washing everything she touched, like King Midas, turning everything to gold. Except the change she wrought was not permanent, for soon after drying the clothes, sheets, and towels, she would have to wash them again, wash and dry, wash and dry, week after week. After her family moved into the condominium with the washer and dryer, her eldest and her middle sisters moved away to college. In fact, her eldest sister moved away even before they moved into the condominium, her eldest sister never had a chance to enjoy its amenities. Two and a half bathrooms, a kitchen with a window for ventilation, new paint, new carpets. The condominium was the first home her parents bought. It brought her immense relief to be living, for the first time in her life, in a home that properly belonged to her parents. The previous year in school, as an icebreaker, her sixth-grade homeroom teacher had had the class fill out a sheet of squares. Each square held a phrase inside it, like "has a sister," or "likes action movies." The assignment was to find a classmate to sign every square. She was roaming about the classroom, again with the illusion of purpose, though secretly waiting for someone to speak to her, her old habits from elementary school resurfacing on this first day of middle school, when a boy climbed on top of a desk and yelled, *Who here is poor enough to live in an apartment?* This was the same boy who, at the end of the school year, after a long series of substitute teachers, would instigate an anarchic uprising against the last helpless substitute. In her memory, he appears only twice. Once, atop the desk yelling, and once, at the end of the school year, diving after their class pet, a white rabbit named Snowball, grabbing for the rabbit's hind legs, squeezing its little body too tightly. She went up to her homeroom teacher and asked if an apartment was the same thing as a condominium or a townhouse. Her teacher said no, an apartment was an apartment, a condominium was a condominium, and a townhouse was a townhouse. She did not know what the distinctions were, exactly, but she did not ask. When her family lived in Bangkok, she heard her parents use the word townhouse to describe where they lived. A townhouse, the house she grew up in, the first one she can remember. It had a small fenced-in yard, two bathrooms, two bedrooms, and a balcony on the second floor, which they would line with candles in October, on the full moon, for the festival of lights. The townhouse also had concrete floors, squat toilets, and cockroaches in the downstairs bathroom and kitchen, but it was a house, built on the earth, with a front door that opened to the sunlight, and she had taken pride in that. The place she lived in the sixth grade, the place her family rented before they bought the condominium, was both better and worse than the townhouse in Bangkok. It had a smaller fenced-in plot of land, the fence built out of wood, and built high, the American way. There was no light but from the sky. Downstairs, there were no windows, and two pillars stood in the center of the space, like the bars of a prison cell, she thought, or the exposed skeleton of some prehistoric animal. There was a single bathroom that the whole family shared, and two bedrooms that opened onto a small balcony. It was not an apartment, despite being very small, and for that she was grateful. She did not have to sign the square. She did not have to admit to her classmates and to herself, I am poor enough to live in an apartment while the rest of you live in single-family homes with green lawns, a pool in the backyard, and large windows that look out onto everything. Some icebreaker that would have been. She does not remember the boy's name, only that their class pet, Snowball, died, that summer after sixth grade, and she always held the boy responsible for the rabbit's death.

And the townhouse on Weyburn Lane, the house that saved her from the boy's cruelty, was also the house that saved her family from their homelessness, their living off of other people's kindness or greed or desperation. There had been another house, near her future high school, where she and her mother and her sisters lived the summer after they were kicked out of her aunt's house. The woman her mother rented from had left the country where she was born

246

for the same reason her mother and father left the country where they were born, but unlike her parents, this woman had the paperwork to prove that she had to leave, and this paperwork gave her certain benefits her parents did not have. One benefit was the woman's house. It did not belong to her, not really, but to the government. Later, she would come to learn that there were houses and even whole buildings like this in her town, where the government housed people with certain paperwork. The woman was elderly and lived with her granddaughter and her son. She remembers playing marbles with the granddaughter on the living room floor or under the kitchen table. Her only memories of the woman's son, the granddaughter's father or uncle, are from this same vantage point, under the dining table, from where she could only see his shoes. The man was the only one who wore shoes inside the house. She and her mother and her sisters had a room to themselves, with a lock on it, just like in her aunt's house, but in this house, there was a small TV in their room, so she and her sisters spent the whole summer watching *Sailor Moon* marathons. She cannot remember why they did not play outside. Maybe it was not allowed, maybe it would have been suspicious to the neighbors to see so many children playing in the street when there was only supposed to be one child who lived in the house. She cannot remember her mother ever telling them they could not go outside, but she does remember knowing that they were not supposed to be there. The woman was not supposed to have renters. In this country, a single-family home was meant for a single family. Once, when people came to inspect the woman's house, in the same way her eldest aunt used to come to inspect them in the past, she and her mother and her sisters had to hide quietly. She remembers sitting on the edge of the bed in the master bedroom, making no noise, making herself disappear. In her memory, the room is dark, it is evening, but they cannot turn the lights on because they are hiding. She remembers her father would call them from Bangkok regularly. On the phone, she begged him to take care of her favorite pillow, Big Pip, whom she had left behind. Her mother had said that if she brought Big Pip on the plane, the airport security in this country would cut him open looking for drugs. Years later, her middle sister said to her one day, *Do you know why Daddy came back? No*, she said. *It's because of what I said*, her sister said. *I told him no and no.* Her sister meant in answer to the two questions their father always asked, *Are you safe? Are you happy? No* and *no*, her sister had said, and she could not remember saying *yes* and *yes*, though she must have said it, must have said it over and over again, every time. She said and did whatever her mother asked her to, because she wanted to be good, because she wanted to do the right thing. Her sister brought her favorite pillow—Small Lay, ironically Big Pip's older brother—along on the plane and they did not cut him open at immigration. Her sister still sleeps with it today, a pillow their mother had sewn by hand years before her sister's birth. Big Pip is decomposing slowly in a landfill somewhere, she thinks, where everything eventually ends up.

For her husband's thirty-second birthday, they decide to drive from the small town where they live to another small town an hour away, in the mountains, where there is a large contemporary art museum. At this art museum, they wander upon an exhibit on light. The exhibit consists of a series of dark rooms that they enter through dark hallways. In one room they enter, there is a small pillow-shaped box of light projected onto the wall and an armchair placed in front of it. She recognizes the pillow shape as the shape of a television screen, a rectangle, with the four corners pinched in. Above the screen, two lights hang from the ceiling and emit a dim orange light into the corners of the room. The quality of light in the room immediately saddens her. She recognizes it with her body, though not yet with her mind. *I was born in this room*, she thinks, *and I will die in this room.* Born, not as a body, but as a consciousness, the way beings are born in the higher planes of the celestial realms. This light gave birth to her consciousness, she thinks, though there is no memory yet attached to this thought, this knowledge. She feels small inside the room, but already very old, as old as she will ever be, like the night she turned ten. She knew then that she had reached the end; it would only be double digits from now on. She knew she would not live to see a hundred. She and her husband sit on a bench in the back of the room and attempt to draw and write in their respective journals in the dim light. Other museum guests enter and exit the room. She hears a woman's voice say, *This one is not even worth it.* A family with two little boys enters and the boys run right up to the box of light. *You can't even touch it,* the bigger boy says, *you can't even put your fingers inside it.* Before they leave the room, she walks up to the light and learns that the boy was right. What she had thought was a projection on the wall is actually a hollow, a pillow shape cut out of the wall, opening into an empty space. The light coming from that emptiness.

In the next room, she remembers what the dim light reminds her of. Her mother, or, more specifically, her mother's bedroom. Her mother, who suffered from headaches and migraines and, later, from vertigo, always kept her room dimly lit. Often, her mother would lie completely in the dark, and it was only when she entered, when she pierced the skin of the darkness, that her mother would sometimes ask or permit her to turn on the single shaded lamp in the corner of the room. A lamp that not so much gave off light but gave shape to the darkness. She does not remember her mother experiencing pain when they lived in Bangkok, does not remember her mother complaining or asking for help. She does not remember her mother experiencing pain when they lived at her aunt's house either, or at the elderly refugee's house. In the same way that she did not experience fear until she was safe, her mother did not experience pain until she could afford to. It was only after her father returned to them and after they found a place to live, and her mother had a room to herself again, a room she did not have to share with three children, that her mother's body could finally acknowledge the pain she endured. Her mother's feet hurt from standing eight hours a day at the cash register. Her mother's chest hurt, because her heart, which had always been weak since she was a child, could not endure the pain of having missed the death of her mother and the death of her brother in a country that was not only an ocean away, but also, more importantly, an expensive round-trip ticket away. Her mother's head hurt from a day spent under fluorescent lights, a day riding buses, and waiting for them, in the sun, or in the cold, a cold that others in this country, this golden state, did not recognize as cold, but that her mother could not get used to. Her mother, who had previously never depended on her, never complained to her, now did so loudly and frequently, and she, loving her mother and wanting to be close to her, she, still a child, would often pad into her mother's dark room, crawl into her mother's warm bed, and, in the dark or in the dim light, attend to the needs of her mother's body, pressing her mother's chest with her small hands, as if resuscitating her mother, bringing her back to life with each push. When she tired of this, she would place her head on her mother's chest, as if the weight of her small head could provide any relief from her mother's pain. Her middle sister had the strongest hands and was usually their mother's preferred masseuse, but when her sister wasn't available, she would rub her mother's feet, her small, delicate feet, as flat and thin as paper. She cannot remember when it happened, when her mother ended up in bed, in the dark room. In her memory there are only two mothers. The mother who was their sole protector, the mother who was always absent, always at work, always moving frantically from room to room, place to place. The clearest memory she has of this mother is of her running after a bus, sprinting, really, with a speed that astounded her and her sisters, who were trailing far behind. She and her sisters had not believed that they would catch the bus; they had already resigned themselves to waiting for the next one. She does not remember where they were going, where they had to be, or where the bus stop even was. All she can remember is her mother's incredible speed, a speed she had not realized her mother was capable of. It was a moment that broke the frame she had of her mother, a moment that revealed her mother's determination, strength, and her desperation, the limit of her self. Her mother could not wait for the next bus in the same way she and her sisters could. She could not believe that the mother supine in the darkness was the same one who had sprinted after and caught the bus. This second mother, the one whose husband had returned, whose family was reunited, who had done her duty as sole parent and who had survived, was motionless. She did not have language for this change in her mother. It was only years later, at the contemporary art museum, when she tells her husband that the dim lighting of the installation reminds her of her mother, that the language presents itself to her. *How long did her depression last?* he asks. *I don't know*, she says, *maybe a year, maybe several*. She resists the word depression. A word her mother never used. Once, while they were sitting in the car in the parking lot of a strip mall, her mother had said, looking up at the pink sky, *I feel things as well, even though I'm not a writer like you*. Her mother felt things, felt them far more deeply than she did, and it was this knowledge, the knowledge of her mother's wordless depth, that compelled her forward. Onto another memory, and another. Her father asking her and her sister to go to the park with him every day after school because he was unemployed. Her father teaching her how to ride a bike so she could get herself to school. Her middle sister telling her elaborate bedtime stories to cover the sound of their parents and their eldest sister shouting. Her eldest sister coming home one night escorted by the police. Her sisters teaching her how to do her makeup. Her grandmother offering English biscuits from a round red tin. The memories are endless. They tire her; she must rest, the way her mother did, so she and her husband lie down on the floor of another dim room and gaze at another box of light. The light is dark brown when they first enter the room, but slowly brightens to neon orange. If she dwells in her dim memories long enough, she thinks, maybe something will lighten in them too. She lies on the floor, feeling the soft weight of her husband's head against her chest, and waits. But the memories, unlike the box of light, do not brighten under her gaze, but grow dimmer and gauzier. She strains to distinguish them, and then she lets them go.

Acknowledgments

I owe this book, and everything else, to my parents. Mommy and Daddy, I tried as hard as I could to preserve a small piece of your wisdom, love, strength, humor, and light, but I know I can't tell your stories the way you do. No one can.

Buds and AKT, I will forever be your loyal disciple. Thank you for raising me by hand and by foot and for always protecting me. I know these stories are yours too.

To my grandparents, great-grandparents, great-aunts and uncles, my brother, all ancestors, thank you for meeting me across the abyss of time, place, and death. Thank you for letting me imagine you.

Thank you to my *saya sayama* at the University of Denver, who helped me conceive and nurture this project. Eleni Sikelianos, thank you for letting a prose writer into your documentary poetics class and for helping me to see the body as archive. Laird Hunt, thank you for giving me the courage to try my hand at writing "nonfiction" (whatever that means). Selah Saterstrom, thank you for your deep care and insight, and for reminding me to ask the text what it wants and needs. And Brian Kiteley, thank you for your kindness, generosity, and unflagging confidence in me and in this book. I would also like to thank Rachel Feder and Frederique Chevillot, for being fantastic readers of an earlier draft of this project.

I am grateful, also, to the extraordinary writing community in Denver, Colorado, where this book was largely written, especially to my magical cohort: Natalie Rogers, my Gemini sister, Mark Mayer, McCormick Templeman, Rowland Saifi, Vincent Carafano, Mona Awad, and Dennis James Sweeney. I miss you all and feel proud to be a part of such a talented and humble pack. Special thanks also to my former roommate Jana and to all my students at the University of Denver and Lighthouse Writers Workshop, especially my memoir and narrative nonfiction students.

Thank you to all the people who helped me make the memories that compose this book: my childhood friends from home, Bryan, Jess, Mel, and Carol; the lifelong friends I made in college, Heidi, Cecilia, Wendy, Allison, Eric, Jon, Walker, Scott, Caroline, and Isaac; my adoptive family and friends in Madrid, Laura, Nico, Ale, Marcelo, Gillian, Nazanin, Sam; and my cohort at Notre Dame, Dev, Sarah, Garret, Jace, and Jessie.

Parts of this book were written at Surel's Place and Millay Colony, and I also owe thanks to Mari Christmas, Jodi Eichelberger, Sandy Shaw, Calliope Nicholas, and to my wonderful fellow residents at Millay Colony.

I am also grateful to the writing community in Amherst, Massachusetts, where this book was finished, and to my colleagues at Amherst College, especially Judy and Anna.

Thank you to all the Asian American and diasporic Asian writers who came before me and created the space for this work. I am especially grateful for Amitav Ghosh's *The Glass Palace*, Thant Myint-U's *The River of Lost Footsteps*, Pascal Khoo Thwe's *From the Land of Green Ghosts*, Chanrithy Him's *When Broken Glass Floats*, and Kao Kalia Yang's *The Latehomecomer.*

Thank you also to my agent, Jin Auh, for looking out for me.

Most of all, thank you to Steve Woodward, Ethan Nosowsky, Fiona McCrae, Marisa Atkinson, Katie Dublinski, and the whole staff at Graywolf Press. Steve, you were my tireless champion through this entire process and I would have never finished this book without your help and your trust. Thank you for an opportunity of a lifetime.

And lastly, I could not have written this book without your love, patience, and support, Deno. You are my one.

THIRII MYO KYAW MYINT is the author of the novel *The End of Peril, the End of Enmity, the End of Strife, a Haven* (Noemi Press, 2018), which won an Asian/Pacific American Librarians Award for Literature. Her short fiction and nonfiction have appeared in *Black Warrior Review*, *Fairy Tale Review*, *Gulf Coast*, and elsewhere, and her work has been anthologized in *Best Small Fictions* and *Forward: 21st Century Flash Fiction*. She is a former Fulbright recipient and holds a BA in literary arts from Brown University, an MFA in prose from the University of Notre Dame, and a PhD in creative writing from the University of Denver. She currently lives in Amherst, Massachusetts, and teaches at Amherst College.

The Graywolf Press Nonfiction Prize

Names for Light: A Family History by Thirii Myo Kyaw Myint is the 2018 winner of the Graywolf Press Nonfiction Prize. Graywolf awards this prize to a previously unpublished full-length work of outstanding literary nonfiction by a writer who is not yet established in the genre. Previous winners include *The Collected Schizophrenias* by Esmé Weijun Wang, *Riverine: A Memoir from Anywhere but Here* by Angela Palm, *Leaving Orbit: Notes from the Last Days of American Spaceflight* by Margaret Lazarus Dean, *The Empathy Exams* by Leslie Jamison, *The Grey Album: On the Blackness of Blackness* by Kevin Young, *Notes from No Man's Land: American Essays* by Eula Biss, *Black Glasses Like Clark Kent: A GI's Secret from Postwar Japan* by Terese Svoboda, *Neck Deep and Other Predicaments* by Ander Monson, and *Frantic Transmissions to and from Los Angeles: An Accidental Memoir* by Kate Braverman.

The Graywolf Press Nonfiction Prize seeks to acknowledge—and honor—the great traditions of literary nonfiction. Whether grounded in observation, autobiography, or research, much of the most beautiful, daring, and original writing over the past few decades can be categorized as nonfiction.

The Graywolf Press Nonfiction Prize is funded in part by endowed gifts from the Arsham Ohanessian Charitable Remainder Unitrust and the Ruth Easton Fund of the Edelstein Family Foundation.

Arsham Ohanessian, an Armenian born in Iraq who came to the United States in 1952, was an avid reader and a tireless advocate for human rights and peace. He strongly believed in the power of literature and education to make a positive impact on humanity.

Ruth Easton, born in North Branch, Minnesota, was a Broadway actress in the 1920s and 1930s. The Ruth Easton Fund of the Edelstein Family Foundation is pleased to support the work of emerging artists and writers in her honor.

Graywolf Press is grateful to Arsham Ohanessian and Ruth Easton for their generous support.

The text of *Names for Light* is set in Adobe Caslon Pro.
Book design by Rachel Holscher.
Composition by Bookmobile Design & Digital
Publisher Services, Minneapolis, Minnesota.
Manufactured by McNaughton & Gunn on acid-free,
100 percent postconsumer wastepaper.